GOOD
DAUGHTERS

GOOD DAUGHTERS

Loving Our Mothers

as They Age

PATRICIA BEARD

WARNER BOOKS

A Time Warner Company

Names and other identifying details, among them geographical locations and professions, have been changed to protect the privacy of the women who generously told their stories to help others. Although all the long interviews were taped and transcribed, some dialogue has been reconstructed from memory and edited for clarity.

Copyright © 1999 by Patricia Beard
All rights reserved.

Warner Books, Inc., 1271 Avenue of the Americas, New York, NY 10020
Visit our Web site at www.warnerbooks.com

W A Time Warner Company

Printed in the United States of America
First Trade Paperback Printing: June 1999
10 9 8 7 6 5 4 3 2

The Library of Congress has cataloged the hardcover edition as follows:

Library of Congress Cataloging-in-Publication Data
Beard, Patricia.
    Good Daughters: loving our mothers as they age / Patricia Beard
      p. cm.
    ISBN 0-446-52359-3
    1. Mothers and daughters. 2. Parent and adult child. 3. Daughters—Psychology.
4. Aging parents. I. Title.
    HQ755.86.B43   1999   98-30861
    306.874'3—dc21   CIP

ISBN: 0-446-67551-2 (pbk.)

For my mother, Sarinda Dranow
For my children, Alexander and Hillary Beard
For my sister, Elizabeth Gutner
And with thanks to the godmother of *Good Daughters*,
Edmée de M Firth
And to its godfather, Peter Matson

Contents

Good Daughters

Models

Mother and I sat for the cover photograph during the summer of 1998. We played an old game, seeing which of us could stare longer without blinking. I thought I'd done pretty well, but on the contact sheets there were a lot of pictures of me with my eyes closed. When the cover was shot, Ellen Warner asked us to turn our chairs around and took a roll of us facing her. This is a frame from that roll. *Photograph by Ellen Warner.*

Introduction

The Train

This was not a dream.

On a quiet summer afternoon, just before my mother turned eighty, she and I were walking across the railroad tracks. Mother was leaning on her cane with one hand and holding my hand with the other, while I tried to restrain our two small dogs, who were tugging on their leashes.

Mother and I and the dogs crossed the southbound track on the cement path near the passenger station, paused between the tracks, and then moved onto the northbound roadway. This was pretty much like crossing a two-lane street on a green light. Then the gate swung down, and the bell began to clang.

"Mother," I said, "the train is coming. Can you go a little faster?"

"I can't," she said, and halted.

I looked south to see how much time we had, and I saw a headlight as the train came around the bend. It was still far enough away so we would be fine if we just kept walking, but Mother had frozen in fear. She tried to take a step, and then she fell.

The engineer was blowing the horn, the train was looming, Mother was on her knees on the tracks—and I was standing there, still holding the dogs.

We were lucky that afternoon: a man on the platform ran out and grabbed my mother under one elbow; I took her other elbow, and we carried her to safety, as the train—a freight, which was not scheduled to stop at that station—moved on past.

Our rescuer helped us to the stationhouse and Mother sat on a bench and lit a cigarette. Her hand trembled on the lighter; the cigarette trembled in her mouth.

"What happened to you?" I asked her.

"I panicked," she said. "I'm sorry."

Mother doesn't like talking about what we now call "the train episode," and I was reluctant to write about it, too. What happened that afternoon reminds us both that Mother is getting more frail, and neither she nor I like to think about that. But the truth is that aging can make even ordinary terrain precarious. We are now navigating that territory together.

What was an almost-eighty-year-old woman doing on the train tracks?

My mother and I had rented a house together for July and August on a small island, a ferry ride away from the New England coast. The dock is on one side of the railroad tracks, the town is on the other. We had arrived at the ferry an hour and a half before it was scheduled to leave for the island because Mother, with two disabled knees and a tendency to get dizzy, likes to give herself plenty of time to get where she's going. Enough time, that day, so we had decided to walk across the tracks to have lunch in town.

The train episode was not the only time I failed to understand how the accompaniments of age have changed my mother's ability to live as she once did. When I invited Mother to share a house with me and my children, Alex and Hillary, who are in their twenties, I didn't spend much time considering how our three-generation household might play out when we actually lived together for two months. Certainly, I knew that my summer would be full. I had this book to write, magazine deadlines, and because I had been going to the island for a long time, many friends there. I did wonder, briefly, what Mother would do in a place where she knew few people and couldn't drive or walk without a companion. But then I told myself that she would be happier in the country with her family than in a city apartment, alone with her dog.

Mother *was* happier with us. But while I love my mother and enjoy her company—and I liked the idea of being a "good daughter"—my sense of responsibility to her and my involvement with work were constantly crashing into each other. Work often won. The children were busy, too. Alex, who is an artist, was preparing for a show, and he had set up a studio where he painted most days, and often late into the night. Hillary was working in Washington and only spent a few weekends with us; when she was there, she was usually out with her friends.

Mother, by contrast, didn't have much to occupy her. She read considerably less than she once had; when I asked her what she was doing, sitting quietly on the back porch for hours, she said, "Thinking."

I felt that I should be better company. "Don't the days seem long?" I asked her, guiltily.

"No," she said. "I'm not your guest. You don't have to entertain me."

That seemed to be true. Evidently, she could entertain herself. I still felt guilty.

Often, of course, Mother and I had wonderful, memorably cozy times together. When the summer was over and we looked back on it, both of us recalled with particular fondness the ritual we developed in the evenings, before bedtime. First, Alex and I walked the dogs through the quiet village. Then he went back to his studio, and Mother and I composed ourselves on the living room sofa with cups of tea and our dogs, and we chatted. Those evenings reminded me of my mother's maxim, "Never go to bed mad," but we were not making up after an argument—we never really argued. Rather, we resolved each day, putting it away, getting ready for the next.

"The house feels alive," Mother said to me one weekend, when Alex and Hillary had packed every bed with their friends.

"None of them treats me as though I'm old," she added. And then she raised the one real disagreement we had that summer. She had mentioned it often. "It's just your book that's making me old," she said.

Mother would surely have preferred me to write a book about any other stage of life (sometimes I felt the same way), but it was because her aging was weighing on both of us that I wanted to write *this* book.

The Sandwich Generation

Good Daughters is not really about me and my mother, except in the sense that we are part of a unique cohort. Our mothers are the first generation in history in which many women can expect to live beyond seventy. Only one in twenty-five Americans was older than sixty-five in 1900;[1]

but now the 33.2 million elderly account for one in *eight* Americans.[2] That is not because there are fewer people in the middle years—as everyone knows, the "baby boomers" still represent the largest group in the population—but because Americans are living longer, and there are now many more elderly than ever before.

While the overall U.S. population grew 45 percent between 1960 and 1994, the number of those over sixty-five doubled.[3] The great boom is among "the oldest old," who are eighty-five and over, a group that swelled 274 percent in the same time frame.[4]

The ratio of middle-aged to "oldest old" has dropped precipitously. In 1950, there were about thirty Americans between fifty and sixty-four to take care of every American over eighty-five. By 1993, there were only *ten* Americans between fifty and sixty-four to take care of each person over eighty-five. Most of the oldest old are women;[5] there are five women for every man over eighty-five.[6]

Longevity surely has its rewards. Imagine how it would feel to hold a great-grandchild or, even better, to be fit enough to baby-sit for her. But the older people get, the more problems they are likely to have with health, finances, and loneliness.

A May 1995 statistical brief from the U.S. Bureau of the Census, titled "Sixty-five Plus in the United States," observed, "As more and more people live long enough to experience multiple, chronic illnesses, disability and dependency, there will be more and more relatives in their fifties and sixties who will be facing the concern and expense of caring for them."[7]

It is already happening, and the "relatives" are most likely to be daughters.

That is why we've added a new title to our vigorous, optimistic nickname, "the baby boomers." Now we are also called "the sandwich generation" because we are sandwiched between our responsibilities for our aging parents and for our children.

We are distinctive in other ways. Our generation is the first in the twentieth century in which the great majority of women work outside the home, regardless of marital, maternal, or social status. As we have loosened the knots that once constricted women, we have also unraveled some of the ties that used to bind us to our families: in the history of Western civilization we are also the generation least likely to stay married.

But in many ways we are *not* different from our mothers or from all the other mothers and daughters who stretch back over time. We still have conflicts with each other, unmended relationships, and unhealed wounds. As humans always have, we still fear old age and death, and as we see our mothers age, those fears are exacerbated.

The way we live—pursuing careers, often getting divorced, sometimes raising and supporting children on our own—is not conducive to caring for an aging mother. When the ancient conflicts that are built into the mother-daughter bond and our deepest fears of decline and death converge with new developments—longevity, a caretaking generation most of whose members work, and the dissolution of the traditional family structure—it is hardly surprising that we should be preoccupied with our aging mothers.

Talking About Our Mothers

In the avid way we talked about men when we were young and about our children when we were a little older, now, in midlife, we talk about our mothers. Among women over forty, these conversations consume more time and attention than I could have predicted ten years ago.

Everyone has a story, yet the anecdotes we tell each other often have a partial quality. Like pieces of a puzzle in a box without a picture on the cover, or phrases of conversations overheard in a restaurant, the context remains mysterious, and the stories leave us wondering. We have so little time to stop and consider the full trajectory of our lives, and the odd details that illuminate the paths we take. When illness, the anticipation of death, unresolved family issues, and the clashes of competing responsibilities hit us all at once as our mothers age, we have even *less* time to make sense of what is happening to us. And that is just when we most want to be clearheaded and openhearted.

These are some of the fragments of lives I have heard in passing, some from women I may never see again, most of whom did not know I was writing a book about mothers and daughters.

On a long plane ride I sat near a woman who seemed to be in her sixties, and after dinner, when the overhead lights were dimmed and it turned out we had both already seen the movie, she began to talk about her ninety-three-year-old mother.

Her parents, she said, were immigrants; her father was born in County Cork, her mother in Vienna. Her mother was a violinist and, in the 1930s, when she first came to New York and spoke little English, she used to go to the Brooklyn docks at lunch hour and set herself up with her violin outside the chain-link fence. Then she would play for the dockworkers, who would drop coins through the fence into her violin case. This was a scenario that was apt to lead to romance, and it did. One of the workers was the man who would become my plane companion's father.

The daughter had been a musician, too. Although she stopped playing when her children were born, she and her mother share a love of music and still go to concerts together.

"My mother doesn't forget anything," the daughter said. Just the other day, her mother had mentioned a Mahler concert they heard in 1952, and recited the entire program.

"She said to me, 'You mean *you* don't remember?' " the daughter told me, with a small, dry laugh.

Something about this remark made me ask if she and her mother were competitive with each other.

"Oh, no," the daughter said, "we're very close." And then, reversing herself, she added, "I've distanced myself from her emotionally, so I can appreciate her without getting tangled up in old issues."

I was disturbed by that daughter's choice to seek "distance" when it would seem that, at the end of her mother's life, both of them would long for closeness. How can a mother and daughter address differences and difficulties more directly, without provoking anger and anxiety?

I was attending a benefit luncheon to honor a prominent philanthropist in her eighties about whom I was writing a profile. There I met the philanthropist's daughter, an artist who appeared to be in her midfifties, and when I mentioned that I had interviewed her mother, the daughter sighed.

"My mother," she said. "She was never there." Then, in an unstoppered recitation, the daughter told of neglect by her parents and cruelty by nannies who knew they could do whatever they wanted because the parents were too self-absorbed to find out what was going on. When this woman was six, she said, if she didn't eat everything on her plate, her governess punished her by making her stand behind the dining room curtains, sometimes for hours. "Luckily, after a lot of expensive therapy, I'm fine now," the artist said.

But how "fine" is she if she needs to tell a stranger, a journalist who is writing about her mother, of her mother's negligence? How can the daughters of not-very-good mothers overcome their resentment and learn to accept both their mothers' accomplishments and their failures?

One clear winter night, around ten o'clock, I was walking my dog when I noticed an elderly woman bent over three full grocery bags.

The woman had a cane tucked under one arm, and she seemed to be trying to pick up the bags, which she had somehow carried this far before she gave out. I asked if I could help her and she agreed. I took two of the sacks and she carried one, leaning heavily on her cane and stopping every few steps to get her balance or catch her breath. During the twenty minutes it took us to walk the couple of blocks to her apartment where, she told me, she had lived for fifty years, this woman complained about her health, the medical establishment, the state of the city streets, and the price of groceries. At last we arrived at her door, and she explained, "It's a fifth-floor walk-up."

I offered to take the bags upstairs, and when I descended, she had just reached the first landing, where she stood, leaning on the railing.

"I wish my daughter was like you," she said. It was meant to be a compliment, but she said it in the same angry, disagreeable voice with which she had complained all the way home.

If the old lady on the street was unpleasant to me, a stranger who was helping her, what does she sound like when she's talking to her daughter? How can daughters manage to deal with mothers who are truly difficult?

These "mother stories" are mined with conflicts, but some relationships between a mother and daughter are so good that the principal issue is fear of loss.

Eliza, an editor, has always been close to her mother. Both women are prodigious athletes, even though Eliza's mother is well into her seventies. Eliza had come back from a visit to her mother and reported that, one day, the two of them bicycled twenty miles, worked out at a gym, and then cooled off by swimming a few dozen laps in the pool. "I don't worry about her dying," Eliza said. "I worry about her physical disintegration. She would be so unhappy if she couldn't *do* things."

How can Eliza and others like her, whose mothers are exceptionally robust and who are unusually close to them, come to terms with change and, finally, loss?

These are among the questions that beleaguer us: How can we address uncomfortable feelings without unpleasant confrontation? How can we make peace with the past?

How can we prepare for a future when we can never again dial our mothers on the phone and hear their voices?

The Quilting Circle

I had heard dozens of partial stories like these, each of them more or less tossed into my lap without much background. What was clear was the foreground: a lot of feelings, most of them neither happy nor fully understood. The stories were provocative, but they were also frustrating. I wanted to know how these women had developed relationships that got in the way of making clear decisions and that blocked their ability to be more comfortable with their mothers.

To get a firmer grasp on why daughters respond as they do, I set out to gather fuller stories, to learn more about the distant past that informs the present. I prevailed on dozens of women to tell me as much as they could about their lives with their mothers and how their relationships evolved. Throughout this book, but especially in the longer profiles in Part II, I tell some of their stories; they illustrate many of the most common situations that daughters of aging mothers confront.

The practical issues cover living arrangements, such as independence, assisted living, nursing homes, and mothers and daughters who live together; financial difficulties; long-distance relationships; and illness and death. Although the women I interviewed came from various racial, ethnic, and social backgrounds, the principal external distinction that made a big difference was financial. Daughters who are worried about how to pay for the help their mothers need or who know that contributing to a mother's old age will make their own more difficult have fewer choices and more to be anxious about than those with greater resources.

The emotional territory on which large decisions and daily life take place is strikingly varied. I heard about deep and unconflicted love and daughters who turned their lives inside out to serve their mothers. But I also spoke with daughters who were angry and resentful, afraid they would be swamped by their mothers' problems. Others felt abandoned because their mothers didn't need them *enough* and the daughters felt shut out of their lives. I heard about competition and criticism and also about the process through which mothers and daughters build mutual respect.

Like most people the mothers did certain things very well and others rather badly. Some were loving and good company; others were demanding, opinionated, or bossy. Some were too involved in their daughters' lives, overprotective, or fearful; others were self-involved and distant. With age, some of the mothers insistently maintained their independence—even at the risk of their health and safety. Others were dependent—occasionally inappropriately so. A few of these aging mothers wanted their daughters to wheel them around. One told her daughter that sometimes she wished she could ride in a baby carriage.

Most relationships are not extreme. The daughters I interviewed usually were on pretty good terms with their mothers, and periods of alienation alternated with times when they were close. But I also learned how daughters cope when they have had terrible relationships with their mothers and how women who describe their mothers as their best friends manage when they become old and ill.

Sometimes, as I listened, I could imagine that if I had known a particular woman when she was a teenager, she would have told me virtually the same story about her relationship with her mother; only the issues they struggled over would have been different. Much else may have sagged and weakened over decades, but the rubber band that operates the push and pull between mothers and daughters is still pliable and strong.

The generation gap between mothers and daughters is, not surprisingly, most apparent in the areas of work and marriage. Very few of the mothers had careers; nearly all their daughters work. Hardly any of the mothers had been divorced; many of the daughters have. Yet, in one respect, our attitudes are in sync with theirs. Even daughters who might well have chosen to pull away for practical or emotional reasons take their responsibilities to their mothers very seriously. I remember how worried many of our parents were in the 1960s and 1970s. They were afraid that we were overthrowing an entire social and moral order, trampling family ties, and tossing our love around to strangers, while neglecting the roots of our real connections. But it didn't turn out that way, at least in regard to our feelings for our mothers. We may be different from them, and we may carry out our responsibilities differently, but we feel as much responsibility for them as they did for their own aging mothers.

As these women told me their stories, I was reminded of the old-fashioned quilting circle, in particular, the one invented by Whitney Otto in her novel (later a movie) *How to Make an American Quilt*. Otto structures her book around a small group of women who make quilts together and, over many decades, talk as they sew, stitching a design that is a metaphor for their interconnected lives. It seemed that the women who talked to me were bringing me their patches so I could sew them into a pattern. The "quilt" we have made together is most like the "crazy" pattern: it has a theme, as crazy quilts often do, but the pieces are lopsided and free-form, rather than neat and geometric. These quilts, like our lives, are vital and inventive, created from scraps—accidents, luck, mistakes—to make humble, but unique, works of art.

What Is the Question?

One morning during that summer on the island, my friend Sally came over for coffee. She was visiting her mother, who had two other houseguests; all three women were in their eighties. We had coffee on the porch, and then Sally and I went for a walk. "Does your mother still drive?" Sally asked me.

"No," I said. "But she lives in the city, so it doesn't matter, except when we're here. How about yours?"

"Only during the day," Sally said. "And she has such bad arthritis in her neck, she can't turn her head, so she can't back out. At night, if she can't find someone to come for her, she's stuck at home. She's game, but she's failing. What are we going to do about our mothers?" she asked.

I have heard that question again and again. What *can* we do?

But first, what are we really asking? I do not think we mean just "Who will drive our mothers?" (Often the answer is that we will.) I think we want to know, "What can we do about the way we *feel* about our mothers?"

Even though most daughters of elderly women who

spoke with me have relationships with their mothers that are on the cusp of being "good enough"—a concept that takes into account the gap between the best intentions and what's really possible—as mothers age and daughters spend more time with them, the daughters find that complicated feelings about their mothers reemerge, feelings they thought they had either resolved or outgrown. The challenge of their last chapter with their mothers is to define for themselves what it means to be a good daughter and then to overcome emotional and practical barriers so they can be more responsible and loving.

Loss is the underlying theme, both for those who can't quite love their mothers without tension and for those who love them unreservedly. Nearly all of us are afraid of the time when we will be motherless. Sometimes we already miss being nurtured and protected by our mothers; at other times, we fear and resent the reverse, that it is now we who nurture and protect them. We look ahead with terror to the time when we may lose our own adult powers. Above all, we experience a heightened consciousness of death, because when a mother dies, her children move up in line.

Why Daughters?

The mother-daughter relationship is like no other. Our mothers define us before we define ourselves. Because we are like them, we look to them for models of how we should (or should not) lead our lives at every stage. Our feelings for each other are unique in quality and sometimes in intensity.

So we are oriented toward our mothers from the beginning of our lives until the end of theirs and, in some ways, even after they die.

That orientation is layered onto the role women have traditionally played as family caretakers. Statistics and anecdotal information reinforce the impression that daughters are still most likely to care for their elderly parents. Because women live longer than men, that usually means caring for a mother.

Other family members are part of the picture as well, of course. Elderly husbands and wives care for each other. Grandchildren confide in their grandparents, spend adolescent summers with them, call them, visit, and teach them to operate the microwave and the VCR and even to navigate the Internet. Some daughters-in-law become the primary caretakers to their mothers-in-law because they are the only women in their generation of the family, or because a daughter lives far away or doesn't get along well with her mother. Sons and sons-in-law manage finances, visit and physically care for mothers and mothers-in-law, and take the heat out of mother-daughter tensions. But even though sometimes a son is his mother's strongest emotional supporter, it is much more common for sons to pay or make practical arrangements, while daughters do the daily caretaking and interact most intimately with their mothers.

In families with more than one daughter, the sisters may be equally involved in their mothers' lives, but usually one takes the greater responsibility, either for practical reasons—she has more time or lives nearer—or because she is emotionally closer to her mother. (In my own family, for example, my sister lives in Arizona and my mother and I live five blocks away from each other in New

York, so I see my mother more, although my sister talks to her often.) Most of the daughters I have interviewed for this book have the most regular contact, the most pressing problems, or the closest bonds with their mothers.

A mother who has raised her children in the same household, with consistent values, and treated them with equal love and attention is often perceived quite differently by siblings who have distinct personalities and needs. When their mother ages, they approach her differently, too. They may disagree about what is "best" for her, and one may be willing to do considerably more for her than the others. A mother's change in status, from independent to dependent, can also unbalance sibling relationships. Although this change can add to the tension, or bring other family members closer to each other, this book is about mothers and daughters, not about entire families. Both in the interest of clarity and because each of our connections to another person is singular—no matter how many other people intersect with that relationship—I have chosen to focus on only one daughter of each mother rather than to discuss, except in passing, the other family dynamics that are affected when a parent ages.

The Good Enough Daughter

Good Daughters is not a handbook, of which there are an increasing number to walk us through the details of nursing home selection, programs for the aging, and legal and medical issues. Nor is this a psychologist's book, although I have interviewed many psychologists, social workers, and gerontologists. My perspective is that of a daughter and a journalist, stationed at the junction where the problems of aging, changes in the culture, and emotional issues between mothers and daughters meet. From the vantage point of that busy crossroads, I have tried to make sense of what is going on and to address these questions: What does it mean to be a good daughter to an aging mother now? Why is it so hard? How can we do better?

In writing *Good Daughters*, I have tried to be helpful, but this book is more about self-knowledge than self-help. Relationships—lives—are complex. The women I have profiled are trying to cope with a range of situations that can't be reduced to one or two issues. The compromises they make are rarely "solutions" in the absolute sense. Rather, they have made adjustments that take into account love, duty, self-preservation, and outside responsibilities—all in the context of larger philosophical questions about the family. In midlife, those questions often revolve around the dilemma of what it means to be a good daughter when a mother grows older.

These are the goals of the "good daughter":

- To help our mothers find meaning and comfort at the end of their lives
- To have relationships with them that satisfy us *both*, and to engage with them as adults, with mutual respect
- To love our mothers as uncritically as we did when we were children—or at least to be better than we have been lately at showing them that we love them

We are imperfect; so are our mothers. We love each other anyway. The psychological premise that children will flourish if their mothers are not perfect, but *good enough*, applies to other relationships as well. We expect so much of ourselves, we "baby boom" women who try to do it all. But if we can let ourselves off the hook—not of our responsibilities, but of our impossibly high expectations— we can relax, and if the tension slackens, we will be able to love our mothers better.

When our mothers die, we want to feel at peace with the way we have behaved. When we say good-bye, we hope that we will be on the best possible terms with each other: a good daughter and a good mother, who may feel great sorrow but few regrets. So we ask ourselves what we can do to help our mothers manage their lives and how we can manage our own feelings about them. Those feelings range from the anticipation of grief—because they will die and we will never see them again—to anger and resentment—*because they will die and we will never see them again.*

While considering the mother-daughter bond as it evolves in the face of age and death, I am also thinking of our children and what they will learn from the way we treat our aging mothers. As I wrote about my mother, I was writing for my daughter, too, not just because it is natural for a parent to want to ease her child's path but also because my generation was responsible for shaking up the social order and changing the dynamics of family life. It seems only fair that we take responsibility for sorting out the pieces and giving our children role models that show how we, too, can be friends and comfort each other, when we grow older.

For all of us—for our mothers, ourselves, and our children—I have tried to focus on problems that can be solved and stories that demonstrate how, together, we can enrich and enhance the last chapter of life.

We already know that there are many ways to have a miserable old age. Why look for despair if you can find hope?

The Mother I Remember

Pat Beard and Sarinda Dranow, circa 1950, in Maine, where we spent our summers when I was a little girl. In this picture, my mother is thirty, one of the ages at which I hold her in my mind.

PART I

Reality Check

CHAPTER 1

❧

The Culture: Some Things Have Changed

"Remember, His Topics of Conversation Are
More Important Than Yours."

Why is it so difficult to be a good daughter to an aging mother now? Partly it is hard because of the changes in the culture that our generation has made. As Victoria Secunda writes in *When You and Your Mother Can't Be Friends*, "Women who today are in their thirties and forties probably have even *less* in common with their mothers than any two generations of women in history."[1] That is true of many women in their fifties and older, too, who just missed being classified as members of the "baby boom" generation (those born between 1946 and 1964) but whose lives are considerably more like those of baby boomers than like the lives of women brought up during the 1920s and the Great Depression.

Women of our generation remember some of the reasons we created a gap between ourselves and our parents. Certainly, we haven't forgotten what we wanted for ourselves when we were young. But while we know what we were running *toward*, it can be hard to recall exactly what we were trying to escape, why we were so anxious to create a larger stage on which to play out our lives—and so unwilling to consider the consequences.

Coming across glimpses of the roles for which we were being prepared in the 1940s and 1950s can be something of a jolt. To remind myself of what those roles were like, I turned to the periodicals middle-class women read when I was growing up: guides for young women such as *Glamour;* chronicles of life at the top of the social and economic spectrum, as represented by magazines like *Town & Country;* and those that reflected the broad middle, such as the *Saturday Evening Post.*

Higher Education

Glamour, August 1960. *Glamour*'s "Ten Best-Dressed College Girls" (a concept that, in itself, indicates what really mattered at the time) were sent to Washington, D.C., to interview the senators from their home states. Each was to ask her senator for a "single piece of advice to a young woman graduating from college today." Senator John F. Kennedy suggested, "Marry a politician—it's an interesting life." Senator Sam Ervin of North Carolina proposed, "Be beautiful, be natural, be holy," and Senator Harry F. Byrd of Virginia advised, "Get married—and you'll never have any problems."

Town & Country, 1950s. A feature story about the all-women Smith College opens this way: "In one form or another Smith College has been honoring men ever since it was opened in 1895. All of its five presidents have been men; its faculty has always had a large male representation; and tradition has ruled that no greater honor could be accorded the senior who wins the annual hoop-rolling contest than that she be the first in her class to marry."

Silly "Girls" and "Women Drivers"

Saturday Evening Post, 1950s cover illustrations. In 1953, a George Hughes cover shows a living room crowded with bridge tables, around which sit mostly portly, gray-haired, middle-aged women wearing hats. At a guess, these women were meant to be about fifty, but only one was slim, blond, and animated; the rest had settled into that sidelined, out-of-play condition known as "matronly." The front door is open, and the hostess's husband stands there, looking horrified at the crowd through which he will have to pass to get into his house.

On a 1956 Steven Dohanos cover, two cars driven by women are halted on a suburban street. The women have backed into each other, crumpling their rear fenders, and are shouting angrily at each other. *Women drivers!* [2]

Home Economics

Ad for Youngstown Kitchens Jet-Tower Dishwashers, 1950s.[3] The image: Mrs. William A. Green, described as a "prominent Dallas hostess," stands by her dishwasher. She is wearing diamonds and a strapless ball gown. The caption: "To me, the care and cleanliness of tableware is a major responsibility."

It wasn't only magazines that conveyed such messages

about the little woman at home. For the past couple of years, women have been forwarding "The Good Wives Guide," an excerpt from a 1960s home economics textbook, to each other via the Internet, with comments like "unbelievable." The subject: how a woman should act when her husband comes home from work. Along with such admonitions as "have dinner ready" ("his favorite dish") are "Touch up your makeup, put a ribbon in your hair. . . . Clear away the clutter. . . . Make one last trip through the main part of the house just before your husband arrives. Gather up school books, toys, papers, etc. And then run a dust cloth over the tables. . . . At the time of his arrival, eliminate all noise of the washer, dryer or vacuum. Try to encourage the children to be quiet. . . . Listen to him. You may have a dozen important things to tell him, but . . . let him talk first, remember, his topics of conversation are more important than yours." This good wife is a model of restraint. "Don't complain if he's late home for dinner, or even stays out all night," the text admonishes. "Count this as minor compared to what he might have gone through that day. . . . Don't ask him questions about his actions or question his judgement or integrity. Remember, he is the master of the house and as such will always exercise his will with fairness and truthfulness." Even, we are to assume, when he has stayed out all night.

Some of this is silly, some is pernicious—and none of it could be published in a major national women's magazine or a school textbook today. That is because women of our generation fought to change the way we were seen and portrayed and the way we lived.

We opened a gap—in some ways, a chasm—between

our mothers, who were well established within the prevailing system, and ourselves, as we launched our lives and a new era of possibilities and respect for women. But along the way, we learned that, just as being treated as living dolls had its costs, independence came at a price. The greatest expense would be divorce and its effect on our ability to provide a stable environment for our children. Now we find that our attitudes and the lives we struggled to lead can also make it difficult to be good daughters to our aging mothers.

The Sandwich Generation: The Facts

The expression used to describe those who are flanked by growing children and aging parents, "the sandwich generation," does not quite cover the forces that threaten to scatter both bread and filling, causing the sandwich to fall apart. Those forces are largely propelled by changes in work and family dynamics.

Statistics dramatically underscore the differences between us and our mothers and the problems those differences can cause when our mothers age. When many of us were born, in the 1940s, only about 10 percent of women who had young children worked outside their homes.[4] With the exception of World War II, when women entered the workplace to fill in for men who were at war, the percentage of women in the workforce remained low during most of our childhoods.

But by 1996, more than 70 percent of the 49.5 million women between thirty-five and sixty-four were in the workforce.[5] Nearly half of them were over forty[6] (which means, of course, that most of their mothers were over sixty-five). If all their mothers were alive, then some 16 million working women would be facing some degree of responsibility for an aging mother.

Women earn substantially more than they did in 1950, when the median annual income for a working woman was between $918 and $1,355 ($5,340 and $7,882 in 1995 dollars). Now the median annual income for a woman who works is $16,391.[7] This is an improvement, but hardly enough to help an aging mother with her expenses. Yet elderly women are likely to need some financial assistance: women over eighty-five are among the poorest groups in the country.[8]

Time and money (too little of both) are not the only obstacles to being a good daughter. Our careers are often at a critical stage when we reach midlife. While some women are just getting into stride again, perhaps after slowing down while their children were young, others are reaching the peak of their working life. Many other women of our generation are rejoining the work world; in the 1990s, 60 percent of the growth in the labor force has been accounted for by women, most of them between thirty-five and fifty-four.[9] If an elderly mother needs attention, the timing of what may be our last chance to restart a career or achieve real success can conflict with another last chance: to be a good daughter.

It's not just the dual responsibilities that can chafe; it is also the disjunction between our attitudes about work and the way our mothers may feel about our careers. Of the many things we want from our mothers, one of the most important is for them to acknowledge what we do, why we do it, how difficult it can be, how good we are at it—and even, sometimes, why we fail. This is asking a lot, especially when an elderly mother needs someone to take her to a doctor's appointment or stop by and bring her dinner, but her daughter is working too hard to get away.

A busy daughter often can't even find the time to have the long phone conversations that may be a highlight of her mother's day—and an interruption in hers.

Margaret, a lawyer, spends a lot of time fielding phone calls from her mother, Sarah, who calls her at the office at least once a day.

When Margaret's father was alive, his secretary had standing instructions that, whatever he was doing, if his wife or children phoned, the calls should be put right through. But Sarah saw her husband every morning and evening, and their phone conversations were usually quite brief. Now Sarah is alone, and the days seem long and empty. She finds reasons to call Margaret at work and then tries to keep her on the phone. (For a while, a consistent theme was that Sarah had misplaced her glasses and couldn't look up a word in the dictionary, so she needed Margaret to tell her how to spell it.)

"Mom, I'm in a client meeting," Margaret says. Then she hears a long silence on the other end of the phone.

"All right, dear," Sarah answers. "I'll call you later." And she does.

"She's lonely, I'm busy," Margaret says. "What am I going to do? I try to be patient and empathetic, but Mom just doesn't understand why my job takes precedence over her loneliness."

Education, or its absence, can drive another wedge between mothers and daughters. We are the best-educated generation in history: in 1996, more than half of American women between thirty-five and sixty-four had completed at least one year of college, but in 1950 not even 14 percent of women in the same age group (which would make the youngest of them 74 in 1999) had attained that level of education.[10] A woman with a college education is likely to have a different perspective on life and a larger scope of possibilities than one who hasn't been formally educated beyond high school. The daughter's education gives her opportunities to work in what was once a man's world, and there she accumulates more experiences that are unfamiliar to her mother, which can widen the gap.

The different ways we and our mothers look at marriage also break the continuity of expectations and attitudes. Women of our generation are apt to value independence over marriage, partly because, unlike most of our mothers, we can't count on spending our lives with one husband. A generation ago, marriage held out the promise of permanent financial security. But with the divorce rate hovering just under 50 percent,[11] marriage can feel like—and be— a temporary condition. If we know we may not have a partner who will share the bills, we must be prepared to support ourselves and, often, our children. And we will probably do it with less than half the family income we would have if we were still married: households headed by women had a median income in 1995 of $21,348; the median income of a married couple's household was $47,129.[12]

Not only does a woman who is on her own have more to do and less money to do it with, but she doesn't have a husband who might have helped her mother financially, with advice, or with some male companionship if she is widowed.

Yet despite the changes in our work and marital status,

women are still the primary caretakers of both young and elderly family members. A 1990 *Newsweek* cover story, "The Daughter Track," cited a 1988 U.S. House of Representatives report that found "the average American woman spends 17 years raising children and 18 years helping aging parents." (The child-raising number sounds low—with two children a couple of years apart, twenty years seems like a minimum.) The story continued, "Three-fourths of those caring for the elderly are women, as it has always been. . . . But today they have other jobs as well. More than half the women who care for elderly relatives also work outside the home; nearly 40 percent are still raising children of their own."[13]

Rose Dobrof, a founder of the Brookdale Center on Aging of Hunter College in New York, writes, "Every study of caregiving relatives has yielded the finding that the role of the care-giver remains a role for women. The reasons for this are easy to understand, even if the role is not always easy to play. Women were the homemakers . . . the ones who were responsible for the maintenance of family relationships, for the performance of *affective*, as distinguished from *instrumental*, tasks in the family. They were the nurturers, the tenders of the ill, the comforters of the unhappy."[14]

Social worker Eleanor Mallach Bromberg agrees. She writes, "The literature supports the view that in average family situations, the child to whom a parent turns in a crisis is a middle-aged woman, either a daughter or another relative, on whom the person counts and who expects to be counted upon in times of illness and other stress."[15] The Administration on Aging has done the math, and they have found that "the great majority of caregivers are women (75 percent)—a quarter of whom care for both older parents and children. Half of all caregivers also work outside the home."[16]

What does "caregiving" mean? Nearly 80 percent of caregivers help with transportation; almost as many shop for groceries and do household chores. Sixty percent prepare meals, and more than half make financial arrangements and supervise other service providers.[17]

Eventually, something is likely to crack when the pressure becomes too great; often, the fissures are seen at the office. *Newsweek* learned from the American Association of Retired Persons that "In recent years, about 14 percent of caregivers to the elderly have switched from full- to part-time jobs and 12 percent have left the work force." An additional 28 percent have considered quitting their jobs, according to other studies. In a U.S. Department of Health and Human Services survey of seven thousand federal workers, "Nearly half said they cared for dependent adults. Of those three-quarters had missed some work." And for caregivers of those with Alzheimer's disease and primary caretakers to *any* aging person, as many as 61 percent take time off work and arrive at work late or leave early. Some 16 percent have stopped working entirely.[18]

Tana, a legal secretary, has a teenage daughter and an eighty-seven-year-old, recently widowed mother, Marilyn. Tana's boss understands when she has to go to her daughter's school for a report or even to a school field day; he has children, too. But when Tana's *mother* calls to announce "an emergency," and Tana has to get in her car and drive half an hour to her house, her boss has been less sympathetic.

"My mother gets palpitations and then she panics. She

calls and she's gasping for breath. What am I going to do? Tell her to get over it? So I leave the office and try to help her calm down. There isn't anyone else who can do it," Tana says. "And when I'm irritated at her because it *isn't* an emergency, I think to myself, What if I were almost ninety, the man I'd been married to for more than sixty years was gone, and I was alone with nothing to do and no one to do it with? Wouldn't I hope my daughter could find a way to be available when I needed her?"

Tana has talked to her boss about her mother. Luckily, she has worked for him for more than ten years, he values and respects her, and he's willing to accommodate her situation. Many women aren't as fortunate.

The statistics and the stories all contradict a theme I have heard repeatedly, that Americans "discard" our elderly. Many daughters are willing to uproot their lives substantially to help their parents, rather than considering their own needs first.

Carolyn ran her own catering business from her home until she gave it up to care for an aging mother. Carolyn lived in a Midwestern city; her parents lived in Boston. When Carolyn's father became ill and was bedridden, his care became too difficult to handle alone for her eighty-two-year-old mother, who was partly disabled with arthritis. Carolyn closed her business, moved to Boston, and took a part-time job in a florist shop so she could help her mother care for her father. Two years later, when he died, Carolyn was confronted with the next set of problems: helping her mother sell her house and finding a place for her to live. When that is resolved, maybe Carolyn will be able to open her business again, but she has decided to stay in Boston to be near her mother, so she will have to find a new set of clients.

The practical aspects of the mother-daughter situation are likely to be even worse for the women coming along. They are having babies later, and soon it will not be uncommon for a woman of forty-five to have two children under ten, a full-time job, and a widowed mother in her late seventies. If a woman who is divorced remarries (as two-thirds of divorcées between thirty-five and fifty-four will), she may inherit another set of children.[19]

And consider this: now that we are living longer and are healthier longer, a sixty-year-old woman may have a job (as nearly 40 percent of women in their early sixties currently do),[20] a sixty-five-year-old husband who wants to retire and travel, and an eighty-five-year-old widowed mother. There is a good chance that she also has a divorced daughter who works and needs help in bringing up a young child.

Work and financial independence, divorce and social independence, and geographic and social mobility create deep divisions between our lives and attitudes and those of women in our mothers' generation. These pressures from the culture—a culture we changed ourselves—produce formidable obstacles to being a good daughter to an aging mother.

And that is before we get to the long and complicated emotional history each mother and daughter share.

CHAPTER 2

The Mother-Daughter Relationship

Push and Pull

Even the best relationships between mothers and daughters have always been complicated. It's not only our own situations or the times we live in that make it difficult to be good daughters to our aging mothers, we are also at the affect of—sometimes at the *mercy* of—powerful and deep-seated patterns of human behavior. Although each generation is different from those who came before, in certain ways that profoundly affect us, we are much the same as our remote ancestors.

The most basic tension in the mother-daughter relationship is a daughter's desire to be close to her mother and the countervailing urge to push her away. Those feelings are not particular to any one of us; they are instinctual and they have biological origins.

It is reassuring to realize that ambivalence is a natural characteristic of the mother-daughter relationship. As I began to focus on this ancient history, I felt lighter—less like a "bad girl" when I wanted to push off from my mother and less singularly foolish when I heard the snappish, adolescent voice with which I still sometimes answered her. Knowing why I felt irrationally irritable sometimes—and, also irrationally, deeply affectionate at other times—put both feelings in perspective and took the sting out of the irritation. (I am always delighted to welcome the swoops of affection.)

A critical element in the way we develop is the exceptionally long dependence of a human child on its mother, which creates an attachment that is more prolonged and therefore stronger than that of most other creatures.

Even very small children experience the push and pull—spurting out in little attempts at independence, dashing back to curl up in their mothers' laps. But because it takes humans so long to be able to survive on our own, we also experience an exceptionally tense intermediate phase, adolescence, in which we both want and need our parents' love yet are getting other signals from our bodies that direct us toward autonomy. In adolescence, although we are physically capable of becoming parents ourselves, we are still emotionally immature and need more experience and information to get along on our own. So we strike out at our parents for holding us back, and then cling to them when the world is too much for us.

Even when a girl and her mother have a natural affinity, they experience this push and pull. In working through the conflicts, one goal is for a mother and daughter to learn to respect each other's singularity. If they succeed, the child is likely to flourish and be both attached and independent.

How does this play out with adult daughters and their aging mothers? Intensely. When the balance is off, even an otherwise mature daughter may experience exaggerated emotions as she continues to test herself against her mother, struggles for her approval and attention, or tries to break free from a mother who hasn't been able to move forward and acknowledge that her daughter is a separate adult. Women who are mothers and grandmothers themselves, well established in their adult lives, still continue to experience the puzzling and often distressing struggle that moves them to feel close to their mothers and also to want to maintain a healthy distance.

This innate push and pull underlies many aspects of the relationships between mothers and daughters. Among these is the predisposition for a girl to relate to her mother and want to be like her. Yet daughters are also motivated to establish themselves as different from their mothers, individual enough to cast their own shadows. An example: any woman who grew up in the 1940s or 1950s is likely to remember the convention of matching mother-daughter dresses. Little girls loved dressing like their mothers, but when they got older they wanted to adopt the styles of their own generation, to look *unlike* their mothers. (There were two unwelcome consequences of the desire to be different: either mothers forbade their daughters to wear what "all the other kids" were wearing or they began to want to look like their daughters—especially in the late 1960s—and started borrowing their clothes.)

Competition is another complication in the interplay between mothers and daughters. It, too, stems from their similarities and differences. It is rare to find a daughter who is competitive with her father, but mothers and daughters routinely compete for attention (often from the father) and about appearance, status, and power. (The anthropologist Helen E. Fisher points out that mother-daughter competition was originally based on the search for food. In primitive societies, she says, their relationship was "one of competition for a limited number of resources. If one eats the nuts, the other doesn't get them.")[1]

An additional ingredient in this highly seasoned stew is the child's need to feel protected by her parents. But protection implies power, and a child who is overprotected may conclude that her parents don't believe that she is competent to take care of herself. Even an adult daughter can feel smothered and weak because her mother is still trying to "protect" her. Or she can feel exposed and weak because her mother *didn't* adequately protect her when she was young or has lost the ability to care for her now that the mother is old. Here, too, the tension reflects the push and pull between closeness and autonomy.

Getting your balance and moving gracefully through this obstacle course is like learning to dance the box step with a partner: one steps forward, the other steps back; together, you move to the side; then you step forward and your partner steps back. But if you lose the rhythm, you may do more than step on each other's toes; you may fall and hurt each other.

So even without conflicts between generations, the wide variation of maternal competence, or personalities who rub each other the wrong way, certain basic aspects of the mother-daughter relationship cause continuing anxiety for a broad spectrum of women. The ties of blood, gender, and membership in the same group and the daughter's bias toward connection pull her toward her mother. Her need to see herself as a distinct, competent adult who can identify not only with her family but also with a group of her peers drives her to seek a certain degree of separation.

The push and pull doesn't necessarily reflect the failure of a mother and daughter to love and understand each other. When we need a little distance from our mothers, we can moderate our guilt if we recognize that we will soon feel exactly the opposite and want nothing more than to talk to them. (This can help us understand our daughters better, too. Instead of wondering what we have done wrong when they seem to be avoiding us, we can relax because we know that an hour after they have said they are too busy to talk to us, we will probably get a long, confiding e-mail message.)

Feeling threatened by an aging mother's needs or her real or imaginary criticisms is similar to the automatic "fight or flight" mechanism that kicks in on a roller coaster: the danger is only simulated, but the adrenaline races anyway. Part of the task of being an adult daughter is learning to leave behind some of these unnecessary impedimenta. Consider that it's like taking the training wheels off a bike, and think how much faster you can travel on two wheels than on four.

Persephone and Demeter

These patterns of behavior are illustrated in myths and fairy tales that were first told thousands of years ago and still provide maps of relationships that are as accurate now as they were when the human race was a few millennia younger. The Greek myth of Persephone and Demeter is a wonderful example of a story that is crammed with common conflicts between even the most loving mother and daughter.

Persephone is the daughter of Demeter, the goddess of all growing things. When we first meet Persephone, as James Frazer recounts in *The Golden Bough*,[2] she "was gathering roses and lilies, crocuses and violets, hyacinths and narcissuses in a lush meadow."

And then, Frazer tells us, "The earth gaped and Pluto, lord of the Dead, issuing from the abyss, carried her off on his golden cart to be his bride and queen in the gloomy subterranean world."

What is a mother to do when her daughter disappears in a golden carriage? Demeter called in Zeus, the king of the gods.

Zeus might not have been of a mind to pay much attention, but Demeter made sure that he would act on her behalf. She turned the earth brown and barren and told Zeus that nothing would ever grow again until he made Pluto give her daughter back.

But Pluto had his own resources. To keep Persephone with him, he had offered her a pomegranate, and she had not been able to resist eating one seed. (Like the apple in the Garden of Eden, this is presumably a symbol of sex and experience.) Once Persephone had consumed the seed, even Zeus could no longer restore her to her mother, so the gods compromised: Pluto conceded that Persephone could spend part of the year with Demeter; Zeus agreed that she would return to the underworld the rest of the time.

The lesson most children take away from this story is that a girl who wanders too far from her mother is vulnerable and may be kidnapped and wrenched away from the world of light, plunged into darkness—and married to Death. But if you read this myth as an adult, especially if you take the daughter's point of view, you might have some other ideas.

The image of Persephone skipping through the fields is a pretty one, but it is not a big stretch to imagine that she is a little tired of this performance. She has repeated it many times, like an actress who has replayed the same charming scene too often, and perhaps she wishes her role had a bit more scope. Demeter may want to protect her daughter and keep her a virgin forever, but that may not be Persephone's preference—and because she is immortal, "forever" gains some heft.

Pluto gave Persephone an exit route from an infinitely protracted childhood. He was also quite a good catch: he was one of the twelve Olympians, the most powerful of the Greek gods; he was rich (Pluto means "the God of Wealth," a reference to the precious metals that vein the earth); and while part of his kingdom was dark, the gloomy part was reserved for the wicked. Pluto and Persephone would have been more likely to live in the region the Greek scholar Edith Hamilton calls "a place of blessedness," the Elysian fields. It is true that Pluto was short on charm. Hamilton reports, "He was unpitying, inexorable," but, she adds, he was "just; a terrible, not an evil god."[3] Since the other gods were frivolous, unpredictable, and tended to toy with women, maybe Persephone found fairness an attractive quality in a husband.

Read this way, the abduction can be seen as a metaphor. Perhaps Persephone was figuratively, as well as literally, swept off her feet.

But the story isn't just a sort of Greek "Beauty and the

Beast." It is more profoundly a description of the time when a mother and daughter must begin to go their separate ways. Surely we can imagine that Persephone wanted to experience a world beyond her mother's sunlit meadows, to be allowed to grow up and establish her own adult identity.

An element of mother-daughter competition may figure here as well. Perhaps Demeter didn't want to be upstaged by a daughter married to a god who sat on a more powerful rival throne. Even crops that flourish are eventually picked or die; in that sense, the Kingdom of the Dead always wins.

Zeus's compromise is a good model for the way an adult mother and daughter work out their connection, balancing their need for each other with the daughter's desire to move forward into her own world.

Myths like this one are reminders that the templates for our own stories are ancient and imperishable and that our own experiences and feelings, locked in the structure of our cultures and our genes, are not our "fault" but are shared with women throughout history.

That a pattern of behavior is old, however, doesn't make it immutable. If we apply an adult perspective to our own stories, as we have to the tale of Persephone and Demeter, we have a better chance of understanding what is going on. Then we can work through our legacy to build a shelter we can share with our aging mothers rather than a wall that keeps us apart.

CHAPTER 3

~

Adolescence in Middle Age

Hot Buttons: Appearance

The tensions between mothers and daughters, like those that underlie the story of the youthful Persephone and Demeter, are usually most dramatic during the daughter's puberty. If the relationship hasn't evolved into a more equal friendship—and even sometimes when it has—the struggle may reemerge when a mother and daughter find themselves spending more time together as the mothers age. The tone in which this struggle is conveyed can startle us when we sound like the teenage selves we thought we had left behind, rather than the adults we hoped we had become.

Often this unstable phase comes as a surprise because it follows a long period during which the intensity of conflicts between mothers and daughters has calmed. The lull takes place when a daughter has left her parents' home and her emotional attentions are directed elsewhere, toward a husband, children, and work. She may think that her mother's behavior has changed. She may assume that, if her mother hasn't changed, at least her own reactions are under control. And since both women are independent, she may have the freedom to order her mother off her territory or to stay out of her way for a while.

But when a mother is old, time is short, and she needs help and attention, most daughters don't feel comfortable about walking away. Forced by conscience, a sense of duty, and love to interact with her mother more than she may have done since she left home decades earlier, a daughter can't distance herself if her aging mother gets under her skin. She is apt to react to their renewed closeness by regressing to adolescent patterns of behavior unless she has found a more mature, less negatively charged way to respond.

A mother can trigger a daughter's irate reactions, with the most intense overtones of adolescence, when appearance comes up.

As it was when we were teenagers, a certain amount of the heat in our conflicts with our mothers now is generated by changes in our own bodies. A women in her middle years, who is perhaps going through menopause, may feel the way an adolescent does, as Mary Pipher describes it in *Reviving Ophelia:* "The body is changing in size, shape and hormonal structure. Just as pregnant women focus on their bodies, so adolescent girls focus on their changing bodies. They feel, look and move differently. These changes must be absorbed, the new body must become part of the self. The preoccupation with bodies at this age cannot be overstated. The body is a compelling mystery, a constant focus of attention."

Pipher goes on to quote Simone de Beauvoir, who wrote, "To lose confidence in one's body is to lose confidence in oneself."[1]

The three times women are most vulnerable to losing confidence in their bodies are adolescence, menopause, and old age. Imagine that a menopausal woman has both a teenage daughter and a mother who has become old and infirm. Is it surprising that the adult daughter will have volatile feelings about herself, about her daughter, who reflects the way she once was, and about her mother, who shows her what she will become?

It is bad enough to look in the mirror and see a face that looks middle-aged, without imagining our mothers standing behind us, showing us how we will look next. And when we see how much we, too, have changed in contrast to our daughters, we can imagine the way our mothers sometimes feel when they look at us.

One evening, my daughter, Hillary, and I were getting dressed together in a hotel room. We had both been working hard and we were exhausted. As we stood in front of the mirror, putting on our makeup, I looked at her face. I could tell that she was tired—I'm her mother—but with a little blusher on her cheeks, she looked fresh, young, and pretty. By contrast, when I examined my own face and then scanned the makeup I hoped would bring it back to life, I realized that this was a rather hopeless proposition. My best hope was that the light wouldn't be too strong when we went downstairs to the party and that whomever I talked to would be more interested in what I had to say than how I looked.

I must have been staring at her, because Hillary asked, "What's wrong?"

"This is the difference between twenty-four and fifty-four," I said, and nodded toward the mirror.

There wasn't much to say about that, and Hillary was

45

graceful enough not to contradict me. "Don't think about it," she said. "Just get dressed and go down there and have a good time."

She was right, and I did, but I haven't forgotten the sensation of standing in front of the mirror, seeing the way I once looked in my daughter's pretty young face, and seeing how I look now.

Hair, weight, and wardrobe are the "big three" appearance hot buttons, and they are all charged with negative energy. Even when appearance isn't the most important real problem between a mother and daughter, anything to do with looks can ignite some of the most instantly incendiary blasts from the past.

You would be surprised—or maybe you wouldn't—to know how often the stories women tell about their mothers, past and present, are related to hair.

In 1997, Emma Thompson and her mother, Phyllida Law, played a fictional mother and daughter in the film *The Winter Guest*. When the movie was released, the two women were interviewed by Katie Couric on *Today*. The principal focus of their conversation about mother-daughter relationships was elicited by a scene in which the character played by Thompson has cut her hair, to her mother's open disapproval.

"What's the problem between this mother and daughter [in the movie]?" Katie Couric asks.

"It's a lifelong thing, but hair comes into it," Law says. "I think everybody relates to that. I mean, Emma once shaved her hair entirely off! And—I was gutted, and it's her hair. And it's her body and it's . . . ah."

"I looked like Nefertiti," Thompson retorts. "I don't know what you mean."

Katie Couric remarks, "It all goes back to the hair thing, doesn't it?"

"It's a very powerful thing, hair," Law agrees.

Thompson, who has said that she and her mother get along very well, then volunteers that clothes can be a problem, too. "If I wear something that Mum's not sure about, she doesn't really say anything. She just sort of looks at me. Like that. You know? And I go, You don't like it, do you? What's wrong with it? So I still seek your approval even though I like to pretend that I don't," she says, turning to Law.

Katie Couric now offers an experience of her own. "When I go shopping with my mom and I put something on, I'll . . . I'll . . . I won't even have it on, and she'll be going [shakes head no]. It drives me crazy. I'm like, Wait. I haven't even zipped it yet! What's your problem?"[2]

There they are: Emma Thompson and Katie Couric, two women at the apex of their careers, and what are they bonding over? Just like the rest of us: my mother, my hair, my wardrobe.

I could fill an entire chapter with hair stories from women of every age. One woman with short, blond hair—very pretty hair, in fact—was having what she described as a "good, close conversation" with her mother, when, she says, "Mother interrupted herself, leaned over, touched my head, and said, 'You've always had a problem with your hair.' " The daughter laughs. And touches her hair.

A woman who lives in Los Angeles says, "I try not to buy into the beauty culture out here, so I only go to the hairdresser for two reasons. One: I need to have it cut and colored. Two: I'm going to visit my mother." Hair is an old issue between this mother and daughter. "When I was about twelve, my mother still insisted that I wear long braids," the daughter says. "So one day, I went to the barber shop downtown and had my hair all cut off into a ducktail. Okay, it wasn't the greatest hairstyle, but it was a lot more appropriate than braids for a sixth grader in the 1950s. When I got home, my mother looked at me and recoiled. She said, 'You used to be so pretty, and *now that's over.*'"

Hair is bad, but weight is worse.

In Anne Rivers Siddons's 1997 novel, *Up Island,* an aging mother and her middle-aged daughter focus their differences on their nearly opposite looks: the mother is a still-sylphlike former dancer; her daughter describes herself as an Amazon. Their phone conversation on the night the mother dies illustrates the power of attitudes about appearance to wound—maybe even, as the daughter sometimes later believes, to kill.

They are bickering, and suddenly the tone of their conversation takes a nasty turn when the exasperated mother says, "I really should have let you study dance when you were little. . . . Dancers don't go soft and thick and puddingy when they get older. They turn into greyhounds, not oxen."

The daughter, in a "red rage," snaps back, "No. Not greyhounds. They don't turn into greyhounds. Have you looked at yourself lately, Mother? Old dancers turn into hyenas. And you know what hyenas do, don't you? They eat their young."

Later that night, while practicing at the barre in her spare bedroom, the mother suffers a stroke and dies. As far as her daughter is concerned, her mother has had the last word; it is that her oversized daughter killed her.[3]

Of course, it's not just in fiction that weight is a mother-daughter hot button.

Becky is trim and athletic; she exercises regularly and has a flat stomach and well-defined muscles in her arms and legs. Her mother, Andrea, does not exercise, but she also doesn't eat much, and she is considerably thinner than Becky. If you were to watch Andrea at a meal, you might suspect that she has an eating disorder from the tiny bites she takes, the way she pushes her food around, and the amount that's left on her plate when the table is cleared—although it is also possible that Andrea burns so few calories that she simply doesn't need much fuel. In any case, she is quite proud of her small size.

From time to time, Andrea packs up some of her clothes in a shopping bag, and when Becky comes over to visit her, she says, "I put aside some things that are too big for me that might fit you." Becky once made the mistake of trying on the clothes while her mother watched. They may have been too big for Andrea, but Becky couldn't button the buttons or zip the zippers and she left (without the clothes) feeling ashamed, ugly—and angry. Now Becky takes the castoffs, thanks her mother, and drops off the shopping bags at a homeless shelter.

Or consider Josie and her mother, Millie. One afternoon they went shopping together. Millie tried on a costume-jewelry choker that sat too low on her collarbone because she had become so thin. Josie watched her, thought that her mother's neck had gotten scrawny, and felt sad. "Here," Millie said to Josie. "Why don't you try it on?" As Josie was closing the clasp on the choker, which fit her perfectly and which she thought was quite becoming, her mother said, "I've always had a swanlike neck. They make these necklaces for women with thick necks."

Another story: Leonora had a hysterectomy when she was in her midforties, took hormone replacements for a couple of years, and then developed breast cancer. Fortunately, the cancer was small and contained, and she was able to have a lumpectomy rather than a mastectomy, but her doctor told her that she would have to discontinue the hormone treatment, which would increase the risk of the cancer recurring.

One evening when Leonora was in her fifties, she and her mother, Bernice, were at a family dinner and Bernice remarked—in front of Leonora's husband and brother, "You're getting quite a 'dowager's hump.'" Leonora had noticed this, too, and was upset about it. "*I'll* never get one of those," Bernice said. "*I* took estrogen." Leonora looked across the table at her mother, who, in her eighties, was frail and stooped. "I could feel something really mean about to come out of my mouth, but I stopped myself before I said it. I don't think my mother meant to be cruel, but she couldn't help herself; she was trying to narrow the gap between us. Sometimes I think she wants me to look old so she won't feel so bad about herself."

The ancient competition between mothers and daughters about looks has been electrified by our own particular generation gap. Among women who fought for a new identity in the 1970s, appearance issues were conflated with the social goal to be different, not just from a *particular* mother but from an entire *generation* of mothers, who seemed to have spent entirely too much time admiring the wallpaper. It is a tenet of the generation that began to make itself heard in the late 1960s that our mothers were considerably more tied to superficial standards—dress, manners, status—than enlightened members of a democracy, or independent women, should be. (The title of the generation-marking play *Hair*, produced in 1968, made reference to the political overtones of that fight.)

We have generational conflicts about appearance with our daughters, too, of course. Tattoos and body-piercing come to mind. But as veterans of the fight between our mothers (white gloves and hats) and ourselves (blue jeans, no bras), we are better equipped to handle our daughters' fashion statements. Even if we don't like the way our children look, their choices don't symbolize a collapse of the social order to us, the way our fashion revolution often seemed to do.

The political battles over appearance that raged in the late 1960s and 1970s heightened our personal frictions with our mothers. We insisted that how we looked was not who we were, and we insisted that how our mothers wanted us to look was who *they* were, who *they* wanted us to be. When the mother in *Up Island* pits greyhounds against oxen, she reminds her daughter that she failed to be the sort of child her mother would have preferred: a small, lithe, "feminine" dancer. Instead, the daughter grew to be six feet tall, broad-shouldered and powerful, a competitive swimmer. Here Anne Rivers Siddons weaves together a personal mother-daughter clash about appearance and social change: by the time her heroine was growing up, Scarlett O'Hara, with her eighteen-inch waist, was no longer the only standard of beauty.

We succeeded in altering the benchmarks of "acceptable" attire and style to what we considered an appropriately inclusive common denominator. (In some ways this was good, in some ways not so good, but it has certainly made it less work to go to bed at night and get dressed in the morning.) Yet even as we claimed that appearance was overrated—or at least that there were many ways to be beautiful—we set another, equally pernicious, cultural emphasis in place, the cult of youth.

By the 1970s, women were far less likely to agree to fashion dictates when it came to what we wore. But instead of what was once called "the hemline debate," we ratcheted up the importance of looking young. The emphasis on youthfulness didn't start with our generation; clearly, women of childbearing age have a distinct value in that they can fulfill the greatest need of any organism: reproduction. In the United States in the late twentieth century, however, there is hardly such a pressing need to reproduce that the emphasis on youth should be quite as hysterical as it is. Yet we *are* obsessed with youth. Our mothers wanted us to be pretty and to dress "suitably," but we ask even more of ourselves: to stop the clock at an idealized age, probably somewhere around thirty-five.

At first, we were beneficiaries of the "youthquake," but the tyranny of the young didn't stop when we got older, and in some ways it has gotten worse. A woman in midlife may be competing with much younger colleagues at the office; if she looks her age, she may forfeit her job to someone who was at school with her daughter. After work, she may be dating, and gray hair may diminish her chance of attracting a man who is also seeing women young enough to give him a second family.

As we are faced with the consequences of our own aging, the penalties of becoming like our mothers take on menacing overtones. It's not just that the popular culture depicts old age in an unflattering light; those who no longer look young are barely shown at all. Women over sixty-five are rarely depicted in movies, television shows, or ads. Sure, there were *The Golden Girls*, Angela Lansbury in *Murder, She Wrote*, and Jessica Tandy in *Driving Miss Daisy*, but what other modern popular heroines are over sixty-five and look it?

There is plenty of material for trouble between mothers and daughters here: the emphasis on youth, replays of old conflicts that are still symbolized by appearance, and a phase in which both our mothers' appearance and our own are evolving. It's not surprising that even a paragon of a mother, who has loved every hairstyle her daughter ever tried, may still push her hot buttons about appearance simply by looking old.

When our bodies change, we can feel as though we (and our mothers) are losing the contours of our personal topography. To try to sharpen features that suddenly seem unfamiliar, sometimes we scrape the rust off the knife and cut with the voice of an angry adolescent girl. Yet the actual problems that can attend old age are challenging enough. What do we gain by spiking them with adolescent reactions? Does it matter if your mother thinks your hair is too short, too blond, or too long "for a woman your age"? If we recognize how many women share appearance issues, perhaps we can disconnect the hot buttons. Instead of reacting, as though to personal insults devised by each mother to keep her daughter "in her place," we can recognize our responses as part of cultural programming we can choose not to tune into.

More Hot Buttons: Inappropriate "Mothering"

Appearance is not the only hot button that sets off over-tones of adolescent angst. Another leftover from adolescence is a kind of inappropriate mothering, when a mother treats her adult daughter like a child and offers a "protection" that is neither real nor necessary. (Its opposite, the abrogation of maternal behavior, can be upsetting, too.)

One morning in the summer my mother and I spent on the island, I drove Mother to the hairdresser and stopped on the way at the post office. "I'll just hop out and get the mail," I said, and pulled onto the grassy verge.

The island is so small that there is only one paved road, with a few branches around the village, and the speed limit is thirty miles per hour. Near the post office, any car is likely to be barely moving. Yet, as I "hopped out" of my car, my mother warned me, "Be careful crossing the street."

Did I laugh at her automatic reaction and find it endearing? I did not. "Mother," I said, in a most embarrassingly snappish voice. "I have two grown children. I support myself. *And* I can cross the street without advice from you."

I was immediately ashamed, but when I mentioned my response to other women, they told similar stories of their own. A frequent source of annoyance is warnings of meteorological dangers. "My mother calls before I go to work and says she's heard it's going to snow, and she wants to be sure I'm wearing my boots," one woman told me. "*Mine* reminds me of the temperature and asks which coat I'm wearing," another said. Their tone combined fondness and irritation—but irritation predominated.

That sort of unnecessary vestigial protectiveness may have ancient roots. "The grandmother hypothesis," which explains why women go through menopause, unlike females of other species, may cast some light on why our mothers continue to try to protect us, when even they understand that their efforts are not needed. The grandmother hypothesis looks back to the earliest time in human history, when women bore children very young, and mothers and daughters competed for food for their offspring. The theory is that menopause was an adaptive mechanism to make grandmothers available to help their daughters rear and nourish children, rather than compete with them. (Grandmothers in the remaining hunter-gatherer societies still provide a substantial proportion of the food on which their children and grandchildren survive.)[4]

So perhaps our mothers, cautioning us about the weather and warning us of dangers crossing the road, are switching a sort of behavioral prehensile tail passed down from our gatherer ancestors. Even when we rarely need our mothers anymore to help us sustain life and almost never need them to tell us to bundle up because it is cold outside, they continue to express their instinct to protect us.

Weather warnings are lighthearted examples. The really tough situations arise when an aging mother gives unwelcome advice or tries to run her daughter's life to "protect her from herself." This behavior was exasperating when we were teenagers and young mothers, but maternal overreaching is particularly surreal and aggravating when an aging mother acts as though she is taking care of her daughter, although the reverse is closer to the truth.

("Your children wouldn't have these problems if you would just stay home with them instead of going to work," one mother announced to a daughter who not only supports herself and her children but also helps her mother financially from time to time.)

Sometimes a mother's "guidance" is part of a lifelong pattern of overbearing and condescending behavior. Yet daughters often set themselves up for such advice and commentary even when they know in advance that they won't like what they hear.

Nicole was in her early forties when her mother, Helen, was dying of cancer. Nicole and her husband had decided to get divorced, and Nicole debated with herself about whether to tell her mother. The problem wasn't that she didn't want to upset Helen, who had always been rather disapproving and distant—she didn't seem to be particularly affected by the ups and downs of her children's lives. Nicole was hesitating because she was afraid that her mother would disapprove of her decision, and since her mother was dying, Nicole would never have another chance to prove to her that she was not a failure. Then again, Nicole hoped that Helen's illness might have softened her and that *just this once* she would tell her daughter that she was doing the right thing.

"Well, I *did* tell her," Nicole says. "And Mother gave me the same kind of advice that had made me choose the man I married—because she convinced me that I couldn't do any better. Mother sat up on her deathbed and fixed me with a look of what I can only describe as disdain. 'Hang on to him, Nicky,' she said. 'Remember: you're no prize.'"

(Helen was wrong. A few years later, Nicole met an attractive younger man who fell in love with her almost instantly. They are happily married, living two time zones away from reminders of the life Helen persuaded Nicole she was fated to live alone.)

The particular poignancy of this story is that even when a mother is weeks away from death, and her grown daughter instinctively knows that her mother's advice hasn't served her well in the past, the daughter still seeks her mother's opinions and hopes for her approval.

Why do daughters unconsciously perpetuate inappropriate or unpleasant interactions with their mothers, as Nicole did by asking for her mother's approval when experience told her that she would never get it? The style of maternal behavior a daughter became accustomed to as a child evokes feelings she learned early to associate with intimacy. Even when that style has always been a source of distress to the daughter, if she hasn't found other ways to feel close to her mother, she may try to provoke her to act in familiar, if upsetting, ways just to make the connection. In part, that is what Nicole was doing—bringing her disapproving mother back from the edge of death. When a daughter puts these old records on the turntable and sets the needle in the grooves, she may be unconsciously reassuring herself that the mother she recognizes as hers is still there.

But as a mother ages, her daughter may realize that she isn't quite as "there" as she once was. A parent who has begun to fail can also stir up childish anger in her daughter, when her behavior reveals how impotent the mother has become.

Lorna, who is a successful corporate executive, says that sometimes she calls her mother and complains about her boss, as though he were a difficult teacher and her mother could request a meeting with the school principal to insist that her child be treated fairly. But, Lorna says, "My mother not only can't rescue me, she worries about my job security and she's afraid that if I make waves at work, I will be fired. She acts like it's my fault when my boss leaves after lunch on Fridays and I have to cover for him with clients. It makes me furious."

When such symptoms of a mother's diminished power to mediate in her child's world kick in, her daughter's anger may be covering her sorrow that her mother is no longer equal to the fight and that the mother she knew is fading away.

What can we do about the way we feel, and how can we disconnect the hot buttons? The therapeutic model is well established. We can figure out what we *really* feel. We can learn what is making us feel that way. We can find techniques to change our behavior and replace automatic, unhealthy interactions with healthy new ones. If we don't allow ourselves to be ruled by feelings that we are ready to outgrow, we can make wiser, more rational decisions about our roles as daughters to our mothers as they age.

Telling Stories

Even the women I interviewed who have successful relationships with their mothers tell stories that are untidy, inconclusive, and filled with conflicts and contradictions.

Daughters often try to contain these unruly elements of their relationship by demonizing or canonizing their mothers, even though flattening the perspective rarely improves the view.

The push and pull between mothers and daughters is innately informed by the tension of opposing forces, and it is further complicated because we commonly experience two contradictory feelings virtually simultaneously. (A simple example is that we want our mothers to approve of the way we look, yet we resent them for expressing their opinions about our appearance.) Ambiguity may be natural, but not knowing exactly where they stand makes most people uncomfortable. To give themselves some relief from discomfiting feelings, many women label their mothers or their relationships with them—for example, as cold, disapproving, smothering, or even "perfect"—and then hope they will stay in their categories. Perhaps we learned to do this from them: in the less psychologically aware 1950s mothers sometimes described one daughter as "the smart one" and another as "the pretty one." But that didn't serve us then, and pigeonholing our mothers doesn't serve either of us well now.

It is hard to resist the temptation to force life to make sense, but it is useful to remind ourselves to be wary of the impulse to impose more logic and structure than are really there or to arrange our narratives into fables that are either too good or too bad to be true. We may want our stories to have beginnings, middles, and ends; themes, heroines, and villainesses; summings-up and accountings—but those are the materials of fiction, more like morality tales than reportage.

Instead of tidying our narratives, we and our mothers can open the constricting seams of the plots we have written for ourselves and each other, so that both of us can breathe. To do that, we must also consider the way our mothers feel about themselves as they age—and the way they feel about us.

CHAPTER 4

⌒

Old Age, the Baseline

First, the Good News

What is it like to be an aging woman now?

Ask Gloria Stuart. She would tell you—as she told the many reporters who have interviewed her—that she's having the time of her life. At eighty-three, she won the Screen Actors' Guild award for Best Actress in a Supporting Role for her part in *Titanic;* and it was she, not the movie's young star, Kate Winslet, who wore a huge blue diamond in her cleavage at the Academy Awards that year.

Gloria Stuart is not unique in her ability to lead a full and fulfilling life well into old age. Georgia O'Keeffe was painting, raising hell, and keeping company with a young man when she was an octogenarian. The philanthropist Brooke Astor was a fixture on the New York social scene and made field visits to programs her foundation supported when she was ninety-five. Dominique de Menil founded an art museum in Houston when she was close to eighty and presided over it and her other charitable endeavors until she died at eighty-nine. Beatrice Wood, a well-known ceramic artist, was named a "California living treasure" when she was 101, worked at her potter's wheel every day until she was 103, and died in 1998, just after her 105th birthday. Osceola McCarty, the black laundress who gave most of her life savings to the University of Mississippi, was in her nineties when she traveled around the United States to promote higher education.

In a 1998 *New York Times* article about the elderly citizens of Red Cloud, Nebraska, a local hospital administrator is quoted as saying, "It seems like 75 isn't old here." Not if you look at some of the local talent. Jessie McDole, a seventy-seven-year-old widow, spends five and a half days a week running her late husband's welding shop. Euniee Fritz, eighty-nine, serves as county school superintendent, a position to which she has been elected year after year since 1974. Helen Holt, ninety-one, "still mows her lawn—with a push mower," a neighbor reported.[1]

For men and women like these, known as "the hardy old," hitting the high numbers means little more than that time is short. Our admiration of them is heightened by poignancy. We know that they are remarkably present *now* but that they are also at the mercy of time, and at any moment they may be gone.

But if you are reading this book, your mother is probably not as fortunate in what she is able to do. The statistics indicate that it is considerably more common for those who live past sixty-five to develop physical and mental conditions that will affect the quality of their lives and diminish their choices.

Not Such Good News

Robert Butler, the founding director of the International Longevity Institute, who won the Pulitzer Prize for his landmark book, *Why Survive? Being Old in America,* reports that 86 percent of those over sixty-five "have chronic health problems of varying degrees."[2] Attitude can minimize the effect of some problems. "About three-fourths . . . of noninstitutionalized persons aged 65 to 74 consider their health to be good, very good, or excellent compared with others their age as do about two-thirds of noninstitutionalized persons 75 years and over."[3] But the problems still exist:

- One-third of people over sixty-five, and half of those over eighty-five, have noticeably lost hearing.[4]
- About one-third have eyesight problems serious enough to impede their mobility.[5]
- Arthritis affects more than half of women over sixty-five.[6]
- Osteoporosis affects 25 million Americans. Of them, 80 percent are women, who lose height, develop dowager's humps, and break bones. Osteoporosis causes 1.5 million fractures a year, of which three hundred thousand are hip fractures.[7]
- Urinary incontinence affects one in ten people over sixty-five,[8] and twice as many women as men. The evidence that the problem is widespread is on display in the stacks of adult diapers on supermarket shelves, but only half of those with incontinence report it to their physicians.[9]
- The prevalence of Alzheimer's disease and other dementias doubles every five years after sixty-five; the

National Institute on Aging estimates that nearly half of those eighty-five and older may have Alzheimer's.[10]

- Heart disease and hypertension affect nearly a third of older people.[11]
- More than 3.5 million American women have been diagnosed with diabetes; this is estimated to be only half the number of women who have the disease but have not been diagnosed.[12]
- Poverty is rampant among the elderly population, especially among women living alone: 44 percent of those between sixty-five and seventy-four, and 57 percent of those over seventy-five have incomes of less than $10,000 a year.[13]

In *Successful Aging*,[14] a recent book that extols the possibilities of living a long, healthy, and fulfilling life, authors John W. Rowe and Robert L. Kahn concede that chronic illnesses prevail among the elderly. But Rowe and Kahn (who cowrote the book at age eighty) insist that such conditions do not necessarily undermine function, even though they can be uncomfortable and inconvenient. One person with a combination of chronic conditions may be in a nursing home, they remark; another may be sitting on the Supreme Court.

That is certainly true, but with each year of life—especially after about eighty—the increased intensity of symptoms and the accumulation of conditions are apt to create obstacles to leading a full life. And for older people whose comfort, mobility, and mental acuity are affected by declining health and resources, their last years can be bleak. A daughter who has some perspective about what her mother may be confronting—even if her mother is healthy and active, but is watching her contemporaries decline and die—can more easily empathize with her and set aside some of the old issues that have separated them.

Isolation and Limitations

When Deborah Perkins, a geriatric nurse-practitioner in Richmond, Virginia, had to tell a woman in her eighties that her memory impairment was too severe for her to drive, the woman "burst into tears and said, 'You might as well shoot me.'" Perkins compared the experience to telling a patient she has a terminal illness. Another woman said she cried when her eighty-six-year old father had his driver's license revoked because he had been driving on the wrong side of the street. "It's demoralizing . . . [driving is] their last grasp of independence," she said. Her father's car now sits in front of his Florida condominium, unused but washed regularly.[15]

As Sara Rimer, the *New York Times* reporter who covered the story, commented, "To have to give up driving is viewed as a step toward dependency and even death." It is also a step toward an isolation that is one of the plagues of old age and, in itself, a health risk. Christine Cassell, head of the Department of Geriatrics and Adult Development at the Mount Sinai Medical Center in New York, says, "There are physical consequences to isolation: people become depressed and confused. All the things that happen with aging are worse for those who are isolated."[16]

To avoid the isolation and lack of stimulation of a home-bound life, some feisty older people are willing to take many kinds of risks. Here's one woman who refused to let a leaking bladder keep her home.

Alexa's mother, Marina, was far from a bathroom when she went to an evening beach picnic with her children and grandchildren and a group of their friends. Sitting on a slatted plastic folding chair, with a blanket wrapped around herself for warmth, Marina beckoned to Alexa, who was standing by the fire and talking to her husband. When Alexa came over, Marina whispered, "I'm going to wee-wee right here," and grinned conspiratorially. "Will you watch and make sure no one sees me?"

"Sure," Alexa said. Just then, a man approached Marina, sat down on a log, and began to talk to her. This made it impossible for Marina to slip down her trousers (which had an elastic waistband), but she couldn't wait any longer. "So," she later told her amused granddaughter, "I just *went*. He never knew a thing, and I kept that blanket around me until we got back to the house."

"I hope I'm as good a sport as Granny when I get to be her age," her granddaughter said.

Of course, in a movie theater or a restaurant, a sudden need to empty your bladder would be considerably more difficult to accommodate, and Marina has had a couple of near-accidents.

"If I have to wear diapers, I will," she says. "But I'm not going to let this stop me from going places."

Isolation is less likely to be caused by geographical separation than the myths about our mobile society suggest. It is commonly assumed that elderly people often live far away from their families, but of the four-fifths of elderly people with living children, 62 percent visit their children or are visited by them weekly, and 76 percent talk with their children on the phone at least once a week. More than half of caregivers have to travel only twenty minutes to get to the person they are caring for, more than two-thirds live no more than an hour away, and 94 percent live within a two-hour commute.[17]

Even parents and adult children who don't live near each other are more in touch than they were in what many think of as the golden era of close extended families, which is often said to have come to an abrupt halt around 1970, if not earlier. Before long-distance calling and air travel became commonplace and relatively inexpensive, an adult child who moved away from her parents might never see them again, and their principal means of communication would have been by letter. Now, for a few dollars a week, we can call our mothers every day. Prior to the development of the interstate highway system, a daughter might have had to spend considerable travel time to see her mother; today the same distance can be covered much more quickly. And with video cameras, grandparents can watch their distant grandchildren grow up between visits.

Still, geographical mobility, even if it is only away from a town a woman knows well, may mean that she has fewer and less solid social support systems. Often those who move are the elderly. An older woman in a new community may not have the chance to develop friends and acquaintances she can trust who will keep an eye on her, so she may still depend on a daughter who may live thousands of miles away. If her daughter doesn't call her regularly, who will know that she hasn't left the house for a week? If her daughter can't stop by and open the refrigerator, who will see that all it contains is a soft, wrinkled apple and a couple of containers of yogurt?

An older woman on her own in a place where she has only shallow roots may also find herself relying on assistance from strangers. Without a social network that could protect her from those who do not have her best interests at heart, she can be an easy mark for unkind or even cruel home aides, dishonest shopkeepers, operators of scams that prey on the elderly, and landlords who take advantage of her. Loneliness and isolation can also make an older person vulnerable to anyone who is nice to her. An adult daughter far from her mother has good reason to worry—and to be vigilant.

Margot, an elderly, nearly blind woman in southern California, was furious when her daughter, Nan, who lives in New Mexico and can visit her mother only once a month, fired her home aide. He was a young man who relieved the isolation of Margot's life: he read to her, took her out for dinner, bantered with her, and watched television with her, giving a running commentary on the images Margot couldn't see. He also offered to take over paying her bills. He wrote the checks; she signed them. Unfortunately, an increasing number of those checks were written to him.

When Nan discovered that he had been stealing from her mother and wanted to turn him in to the police, Margot refused. And now that her companion is gone, Margot still misses him. It was better to live with an amusing, thoughtful felon, she says, than to be stuck at home with her current aide, a kindly older woman who doesn't speak much English and who provides care but not much company.

Another aspect of age that can isolate even active and healthy older people is fear of being an easy target for crime. The elderly, especially women, are often afraid they will be mugged, even though the statistics show that white women over sixty-five have the lowest victimization rates for violent crime: 3 percent.[18] But knowing something is unlikely to happen doesn't necessarily help. A woman who walks slowly and is not strong enough to defend herself thinks carefully about where she goes and often avoids going out, especially at night, unless she is accompanied by someone younger and stronger—such as her daughter. One of the reasons for the low victimization rate may even be that older women stay home to avoid exposing themselves to situations in which they may be vulnerable.

The most immediate reason that older people are lonely is because so many members of their own age group have died. "The constant companion of old age is loss and grief and efforts to make restitution for those losses," Robert Butler says.[19] The actual losses that punctuate age are exacerbated by the *anticipation* of loss. "I don't know any woman, unless she's fifteen years older than her husband, who doesn't think about the fact that she is likely to be the survivor," Rose Dobrof of the Brookdale Center on Aging says. "Women live longer than men and most of us marry men who are older than we are. So we can't say 'if' anything happens: it's usually 'when.' "[20]

Along with the loss of a husband comes the depletion of a generation of irreplaceable friends, siblings, and cousins. And after a woman is widowed, she faces another loss: of her potential for finding a new mate. While we've all heard stories of romance and marriage after seventy, the percentage of women who remarry at that stage of life is very low: too few men are left, and those who survive are usually celebrating their fiftieth wedding anniversaries. (More than 65 percent of women seventy-five and over are widowed, as compared with less than a quarter of men in the same age group.)[21] The scarcity of men doesn't just affect a woman's chances for remarriage; she is also likely to spend what feels like an unnatural proportion of her life without the company of men of her own generation.

Of the many difficult situations an older person is likely to encounter, isolation is the one a good daughter has the most power to alleviate. Even a little companionship, regular phone calls, and any kind of attention that provides stimulation and a sense of connection to the outside world are often disproportionately helpful, considering the modest amount of time and effort they require.

Loss and Stress

Robert Butler has written that "older persons experience more stresses than any other age group, and these stresses are often devastating. The strength of the aged to endure crisis is remarkable, and tranquillity is an unlikely as well as inappropriate response under these circumstances."[22] It is not surprising, then, that depression is a frequent traveling companion of the elderly. So is fear of dementia: even an inconsequential diminution of brainpower can be confusing, depressing, and frightening. The widespread publicity about Alzheimer's disease in recent years has helped those who suffer from the disease and their families but heightened the anxieties of those who have considerably less disabling impairment (or whose mental acuity is temporarily blunted by medications). They may have lost only a little function, but their clarity can be further affected by fear that they are about to descend into deep darkness.

Rose Dobrof says that five years ago, when she was in her late sixties, she might have identified the narrowing of opportunity as one of the worst attendants of age. "Now I would place more emphasis on loss. The ultimate betrayal is that the body aches and decays and dies. So first there's the awareness of physical loss," Dobrof says, adding that she recently (and reluctantly) retired from playing tennis and gave her racket to a grandchild.[23]

Women lose more than health and physical ability. Losing their looks is inevitable, or at least it is perceived that way in our culture, where attractiveness and youth are inextricably paired. The more beautiful a woman was when she was younger, the more likely she is to be distressed by the visible signs of age. Some mothers react by ratcheting up competition about appearance with their daughters. Others retreat and stay out of sight. When one of the most famous actresses of the century could no longer hide the way age had changed her, first she refused to have her picture taken, and then she refused to leave her house because she was afraid paparazzi might snap her photo. Another beauty, who, year after year, had been named the best-dressed woman in the Texas city where she lived, began to lose her eyesight in her early sixties. Her daughter says that she wouldn't even allow members of her family to take her picture. "Mom hated it that she couldn't see how she looked before she got in front of the camera. And if she *had* allowed her picture to be taken, she couldn't see well enough to inspect the prints, choose the best of them, and tear up the others."

Christine Cassell comments, "In this society, to be a successful woman is to be attractive. What happens when you become a 'little old lady' and people don't even see you on the street anymore?"[24]

A particularly bitter loss is of the central position in the family. "We have to accept that we are no longer the stars in our children's family dramas, and that their spouses and children come before us—as they should," Dobrof says.[25] For most mothers, this shift begins when their children get married, although many still maintain a "maternal" role because they are still active in community affairs or business and can provide introductions and advice that underscore their seniority. The symbol of being at the head of the family—if not at its daily center—is sustained when a mother continues to be the hostess for birthday, holiday, and other special gatherings. Baby-sitting for young grandchildren, which may provide the crucial assistance that allows her daughter or daughter-in-law to work, also helps an older woman feel needed—because she is. As long as a mother can spin her Rolodex and turn up a useful phone number, cook Thanksgiving dinner, or solve family problems such as how to reduce a child's fever, she will not feel marginalized in her children's lives. She may even welcome the change to a relationship in which her children are involved with her in a less dependent way. But then a small event can suddenly make a mother feel as though she is no longer in charge or even useful. The attendant sense of loss can be devastating. For example, a mother who turns over hosting a family event to her daughter or daughter-in-law may suddenly feel that, rather than being the matriarch of the family, she has been demoted to just another guest.

Sylvia, an indomitable and energetic woman in her late seventies, had recently moved to an assisted-living residence, where she could no longer hold her traditional Christmas dinners. Her son and daughter-in-law suggested that they should be the headquarters for the family celebration because they had the youngest children, and Sylvia agreed.

A couple of weeks before Christmas, Sylvia called her daughter-in-law and told her that the holiday wouldn't "feel right" unless she cooked the turkey, so she had decided to bring it with her. To do this, Sylvia got up at five in the morning, half-cooked a twenty-pound turkey, enlisted a nurse at the residence to pack it into the trunk of her car, and drove the hour and a half to her son's house. There, he unloaded the turkey and put it in the oven his wife had preheated according to Sylvia's instructions. Sylvia basted the turkey, made her delicious gravy, and was able to feel that, in the same way that the turkey was the centerpiece of the meal, she was still, symbolically at least, the most indispensable "ingredient" of the day.

One loss that can affect every aspect of an older person's life is lack of money. A consequence of the unprecedented longevity that has increased the elderly population so dramatically is that women who in their early seventies had enough money to support themselves for five or ten years often outlive their resources. The decline in financial independence is connected to another upsetting situation: loss of status. Whether a woman gained standing through her husband's job or her own paid or volunteer position, she can lose job-related status (and interaction and stimulation) when she or her husband retires or her husband dies. The depletion of financial resources and the loss of the chance to be useful through a job, community service, or helping other family members have emotional consequences, too. The most common is depression, but anger is another understandable reaction to being marginalized.

Although stories of exceptional people who lead healthy, fulfilling lives are heartening, the motif of most elderly women's lives is more likely to be an inevitable series of losses: of health and physical prowess, looks, the central role in the family, husband and friends, and, finally, her life. To cope with these losses and grow through them calls for a brave heart, a philosophical outlook—and a good daughter.

CHAPTER 5

~

What Mothers Want

"I'm Not Old"

During the summer my mother and I spent together, one of our ongoing topics of conversation was what to call her stage of life. All summer, she fulminated when I said "old age" or "elderly."

"I am not old," she would insist. (Evidently, it is not just baby boomers who feel that, by denying age, we can beat it off.) Finally, I asked Mother to help me find another term, but despite many attempts, we were unsuccessful. We tried "fourth quadrant," "fourth season," "closing the circle," and "stage of development"—all terrible.

"But I don't feel old," Mother said. "Look at your father. *He* never got old."

That was true. My father went to his office one day; in the evening he played cards, as he had every Monday night for as long as I could remember. Then he came home, went to bed, had a massive heart attack, and never woke up. Before the men from the funeral home came to take his body away, I went to my parents' apartment to see him. Daddy was lying peacefully on his back, with his hands crossed over his chest, the way he always slept. He looked satisfied and peaceful. He had gotten his way: he said he wanted to "die with his boots on," and he did. Daddy lived to be eighty, but he wasn't "old."

One evening at dinner that summer on the island, Mother engaged my son, Alex, in the "what to call old age" discussion. By then, she was getting desperate enough to have suggested "twilight" and "day's end."

"How about this?" Alex said. "There's a pie," he started—I could tell he was about to make up something as he went along. "When you haven't cut into it yet, the crust is crisp and the fruit is tart, and it hasn't started to get runny. Then you begin to eat it, and after a while the fruit gets mushy and the crust starts to flake, and maybe it gets a little moldy . . ."

"I'm not moldy," Mother said, laughing.

"Of course not," Alex said. "But that slice is still sweet, and it tastes good, so you really enjoy the last piece because you know there isn't any more."

That was a nice diversion but hardly a solution.

"I don't like this book," Mother said—again. "You're making me old."

"When do you think old age begins?" I asked her.

"Not yet," she said.

(This attitude is not unusual. In studies of people over eighty, 60 percent said they did not think of themselves as "old.")[1]

Certain characteristics carry so much weight in our culture that they can overwhelm other qualities. Among these are illness, sexual orientation, skin color—and age, both young and old. Our mothers are aging, but they are also many other things: smart or not so smart, funny or serious, generous or stingy. To throw the blanket of age over them is to deprive them of their individuality—and sometimes to compromise their independence because they are seen as too frail to take care of themselves or make their own decisions. These are good reasons for women like my mother to resist being categorized. Many older people are well aware of the danger of being compressed into someone else's idea of what it means to have passed certain birthdays; some of them are quite successful at avoiding situations in which they can be stereotyped and robbed of their autonomy.

When Lily, 81, was diagnosed with a brain tumor at home in New Jersey, her daughter, Genevieve, who lives in Houston, proposed that Lily come to Texas for a second opinion. Lily agreed that was a good idea and flew to Houston to see a specialist Genevieve found for her. "I offered to go to the doctor with her when she got here," Genevieve says, "but my mother said, 'No. I want to go by myself. If you're there, he'll talk right over me, to you. It's my brain and I want to use it as long as I can.'"

Lily is still using her brain: the tumor was benign and operable, and that Christmas Genevieve and her husband invited her to join them and their children on their annual skiing trip in Colorado. "We arranged a direct flight, so Mother wouldn't have to change planes," Genevieve reports. "But there was a problem with the landing gear. The plane was rerouted to Denver, had to drop its fuel, and landed on its belly. Mother said she was the calmest person on the aircraft. People were crying and throwing up, but she said, 'I thought, I've made it this far in my life, and I'll probably make it to Vail.'"

The Abkhasian people of the Caucasus, who are known for their longevity, speak of their elderly as "long-living,"[2] which is certainly a more positive view. "Late life" isn't bad either; sort of like "midlife," which sounds less laden than "middle-aged." But one thing we both know is that, by any name, age is the breeding ground for conditions that threaten something else that most of our mothers are trying to maintain: their independence.

Independence

Older people commonly want what younger people want: to be independent. "Part of the American ethos is independence and individualization," Robert Butler of the International Longevity Institute says. "A lot of older people, in a sense, don't really want anything from their daughters. They want to live by themselves and even when they become demented, they will be angry with a daughter who tries to dress them in the morning."[3]

Those who resist assistance may be preserving their own well-being, as Butler inferred from a study he mounted in the 1970s of two groups of elderly people in similar circumstances. One group received a little extra assistance with the activities of daily living, in the hope that the help would enable them to stay out of residential care. The control group did not receive any special assistance. To Butler's surprise, those who received *no* help thrived longer on their own, while those who were assisted became weaker sooner.[4]

Myrna I. Lewis, a social worker who is married to and collaborates with Robert Butler, has coined the phrase "responsibly dependent" for a stage in which a parent retains as much independence as possible while accepting necessary support.[5] Rose Dobrof, of the Brookdale Center on Aging, elaborates: "We don't want to be a burden, and we know that people do not love burdens," Dobrof says. "But on the other hand, we want to know that we can rely on our daughters when we need them." Another way this has been described, she says, is "intimacy at a distance."[6]

That's what Edith, a hearty eighty-one-year-old, insists on. "Tell women your age they nag us too much," she says. Edith prefers her winters in New York, where she lives by herself in an apartment, to her summers on Cape Cod with six children and thirteen grandchildren. She explains that she likes having her family around, but either they rush past her on the way to tennis, sailing, or cocktails or one of them suddenly settles down on a sofa, looks earnestly at her, and says, "Now, Mother, have you considered what you would do if you couldn't live on your own anymore?"

"Of course I have," she answers tartly. "And I'll worry about that when I have to. If I lose my marbles, you'll put me in a nursing home, where I belong. But don't push me into senility."

When an elderly woman insists on continuing to live on her own, it doesn't necessarily mean that she is denying her vulnerability. She may have made a clear-eyed decision to retain her privacy and independence, and she may be willing to pay the price—even if she might have a stroke and lie on the floor for hours before anyone finds her.

What about guilt? Won't daughters feel even guiltier if we do less, rather than more, for our mothers? Not if we understand that we are respecting their autonomy and that often our guilt is a symptom of inflated, unrealistic, and sometimes intrusive expectations, rather than a response to what our mothers need or want from us. "Beware of overdaughtering," says Robert Butler. One approach to "What shall we do about our mothers?" is, Not too much and not too soon.

Sometimes a mother's insistence on "independence" can make her more dependent on her daughter. In New York City, an older woman or man is often accompanied by a "walker," a hired attendant. But some older people feel these companions are too much like nurses and compromise their autonomy. Although few daughters have the time or inclination to take their mothers for daily walks, sometimes they do it anyway or find other ways to support their mothers' desire for independent locomotion.

Ellen's mother, Nancy, at ninety-five, insisted on loping around town with a canvas tote bag on her arm, either walking or taking the bus. When Nancy began to scramble street and building numbers and to set out for one destination and end up, slightly puzzled, at another, Ellen tried to persuade her to hire a walking companion. Nancy refused, so Ellen came up with a solution that Nancy either didn't notice or was able to overlook. Ellen, who lives only a few blocks away, calls her mother every morning and finds out what her plans are. If Nancy is going any farther than the grocery store on the corner, Ellen says that she is on her way to an appointment and offers to pick up her mother in a taxi and drop her off "on her way."

These days, Ellen's "appointment" is most likely to be with Nancy. To make it possible for her mother to retain the sense that she is independent, Ellen has suspended her volunteer work.

"This could go on for a while," Ellen says. "My mother's *grandmother,* who was a teenager during the Civil War, was a hundred and three when she died. But maybe if I live as long and give my children as little trouble as my mother has given me, they'll help me get around on my own."

Meanwhile, when someone mentioned to Nancy how attentive Ellen is, Nancy snapped, "I don't want attention. I do just fine on my own."

Worrying about a mother's safety can push a daughter to interfere more openly than Ellen has done. When an adult daughter starts telling her mother what to do, her suggestions are likely to activate a maternal version of "hot buttons." A mother who feels that her daughter is depriving her of the opportunity to make decisions about her life may protect herself through direct attacks, guerrilla warfare, or deception about a medical condition because she is afraid her daughter will use her vulnerability to take over.

Daughters hear their most grating teenage voices emerging from their middle-aged selves when mothers hit *their* hot buttons, but mothers can also be provoked to reenact their part in the old adolescent power plays. Alas, the dramatic material is still available, and mothers whose daughters become too bossy resuscitate long-disused techniques to remind them who is the parent. But neither mother nor child needs to dominate when they both act like adults and don't threaten each other's autonomy.

*   *   *

What happens when an older person no longer can be independent or even participate in the life around her? A responsible daughter doesn't have much choice in some situations and must step in and make decisions if her mother becomes mentally or physically disabled or is just too frail to take care of herself. Even the most considerate and tactful daughter is likely to find herself the target of her mother's anger then, and sometimes she has to take the heat and do the best she can.

CHAPTER 6

~

The Opportunities of Old Age

Growth

In the natural order of life, humans decline in many ways, but there are clear indications that we can also continue to grow and refute the pervasive cultural constructions that treat the last quadrant of life as an inexorable degeneration. With age, people do not inevitably become like the figures in an old photograph, exposed to sun until the faces have faded and the people look like ghosts. For some, the last phase is another period of development, one that has been overlooked because so many of our current values are calibrated in the context of more: more money, more power, more miles per gallon, more karats—if not more years on the planet.

Age does not have to be all loss. When people lose their sight, they develop other faculties; certain abilities do diminish in old age, but others can grow stronger.

What can we expect of our mothers at this stage of their lives?

My mother and I talked about this one night. "To make the best of the situations we're in," Mother said.

Could that include growth, as well as coping with decline?

"I don't see why not," she said.

When I think of growing, I think of children and the days when my friends and I discussed them as we sat on park benches or on stools in each other's kitchens. We helped each other guide our children through the stages of development that would lead them to succeed in school, make friends, prepare themselves for fulfilling work, find loving partners, and eventually be good parents themselves.

But what are we helping our mothers prepare for? Surely to adapt to what has changed and is still changing—and maybe to do more than that. Robert Butler calls *mental health* "the capacity to thrive rather than just survive" and adds, "There are many ways to be emotionally healthy in old age, but several common themes emerge: the desire to be an active participant, to make one's own decisions, and to share mutual love and respect with others."[1]

"A major task in late life is learning *not* to think in terms of a future," Butler writes. "A satisfying resolution is found among those elderly who begin to emphasize the quality of the present time remaining rather than the quantity . . . a sense of immediacy, of here and now, of living in the moment."[2] Members of our generation who have tried to incorporate Eastern philosophies of "living in the moment" into our lives will recognize that anyone who has managed to succeed at this formidable challenge is surely demonstrating signs of growth.

At any stage, we can encounter new situations that spur development, and rising to the occasion may reveal great reserves of strength, adaptability, and new interests. Among

the "growth opportunities" for many older women is coping with the death of a husband. My mother is one of the
women who met the challenge of making a new life for
herself after her seventieth birthday or, to be precise, a
few weeks before it, when my father died.

For the first time, Mother lived alone—unless you count
her dog, whose company had its depressing aspects.
Each evening at six, my mother listened to the dog trot-
ting down the hall, toenails ticking on the wood floor.
Then Mother would hear a low thump and sigh, as the
dog settled in a heap by the front door to wait for my father to come home from work. When the elevator
stopped outside the door and the afternoon newspapers
arrived instead of Daddy, the dog picked herself up and,
with her tail slung low, slowly and sadly walked back
down the hall to slump on her pillow on the floor of my
mother's bedroom.

Mother had never worked in an office, but she managed to sell my father's business. She sold the apartment
where my sister and I had grown up, bought a smaller
apartment, and invested the difference so she would
have income to live on. She continues to volunteer at the
hospital two days a week and serves on an active board
there. When she couldn't cry after my father died, she
signed up with a psychiatrist for grief counseling and
still sees him from time to time.

This doesn't sound like winding down or leaning on her
children; it sounds like growth. For a while, though, my
sister and I didn't recognize what Mother was doing for
herself. We were waiting for her to fail, to need us, to com-
pel us to strip off great swaths of our own lives like peels

of skin to graft onto her so we could help our mother find a way to lead her life.

Mother has gained strength from the ten years she has spent on her own and the lessons she has learned, not least of which is how well she can do by herself. That experience will serve her well as she moves into the next phase. Perhaps then we will have to make some adjustments in our relationship. But if the last decade is any indication, Mother will probably grow in other ways until the end.

Life Review

"Only in old age can one experience a personal sense of the entire life cycle," Robert Butler says. An aspect of this experience is "a broadening perspective. . . . One comes, in part at least, to know what life is all about."[3] Gaining a sense of perspective is harder in the bustle of midlife, but when we have lived through most of the life cycle, a common tendency is to engage in what many speak of as "life review." Some do this in an orderly, outspoken way; for others, it is more like background music. Although we tend to review our lives at all the milestone birthdays that end with a zero or a five, there is more to look back on and less chance to remedy mistakes as we move into the bigger numbers. "The notion that you can enter old age with no regrets is foolish," Rose Dobrof says. "The question is to what extent you can do business with your regrets and put them down a little bit."[4]

Life review can be stimulated by looking through old scrapbooks and photo albums, alone or with a family member or friend. I stumbled on this technique by accident myself the last time I saw my mother-in-law before she died.

"Mrs. B" (she was loving and generous, but she believed in a certain generational formality, which did not involve calling one's elders by their first names) was my former husband's mother. He and I have been divorced for many years, but I have remained good friends with him and his family. Our bonds have surely been strengthened because his mother, who had three sons and no daughter, obdurately refused to lose the daughter-in-law to whom she was closest. "You can divorce each other," she told me, "but you can't divorce me."

Although Mrs. B suffered from dementia in her last years, she retained a sense of "connectedness" that overrode her mental lapses. One summer evening shortly before she died, I took the train to Long Island, where she and my father-in-law lived, to have dinner with them and spend the night. After dinner, when Mr. B had gone to bed, I proposed to my mother-in-law that she and I look through the photograph albums she had kept from the time she was first married until her sons were grown. She couldn't remember where she had put them, but I searched through her cupboards and finally found the books. Then we sat across from each other at a card table in the living room, sorted the albums chronologically, and, starting with the 1930s, began to work our way through her life.

All that evening, as she talked about events and told anecdotes that the pictures recalled for her, she was sharp and funny and dry—just the way she had once been.

I felt sad when I closed the last album, but that was because we had had such a good time together and it was over, not because of anything the pictures and their stories revealed. They showed a woman who had been a lively and involved mother, a remarkable athlete, and who had a lot of fun. I had a sense that she was passing something along to me—"Here is what it was like and what it added up to"—not explicitly, but in an instinctual way. I wished that my children could have been there.

My mother-in-law was far from physically demonstrative, but the next morning, before I took the train back to the city, I went into her room and sat on the edge of her bed—she no longer arose at seven, as she had for most of her life—and we hugged each other and said goodbye.

That was the last time I saw her. A few days before her seventy-ninth birthday, Mrs. B died suddenly, at home, with a nurse to hold her hand. I heard the news in an airport when I called my office. I put on my sunglasses to hide my tears—Mrs. B would not have liked to think of me crying in public—and sat on a bench. There, as she and I had done together, I reviewed the images of her life. The one I liked best showed her on a bicycle during the Second World War, when gas was rationed and she pedaled around Long Island with her littlest son in a basket and the two older boys trailing behind on their first two-wheelers.

When my mother's eightieth birthday approached, I thought of the evening of the photo albums. My sister and my children and I borrowed the huge "picture box" in which Mother had stashed pounds of photos and memorabilia, including an old dance card, letters, and family documents. We emptied out the box on sofas and table-tops in my apartment and chose the best photographs to make an album of Mother's life. As we were working on it, my children asked me questions about the pictures and memorabilia; they reminded me that it is not just some-one at the end of her life who is interested in considering the past, how it led toward the present, and what it means for the future. Our project in family history jump-started all of us to begin asking Mother about people who died and things that happened before we were born. As the only remaining grandparent, she is the last witness to the experiences of our immediate family.

Mother keeps her album on a desk in her living room, browses through it, and shows it to her friends. From time to time, she says, "I was looking at my album and I re-membered . . ." and then she tells me a story. "My favorite birthday present," she calls it, although eighty certainly wasn't her favorite birthday.

CHAPTER 7

A Role Reversal?

Role reversal: I've heard it over and over again. The idea is that, at a certain point, a daughter becomes her mother's mother. This defies logic and experience: life is not like a car that goes backward and forward when you shift gears. The concept is so pervasive, though, that both mothers and daughters can buy into it.

Roberta's mother, Joyce, has done everything she can to preserve the illusion that she is still young. She had a face-lift in her early seventies, and she is learning tae kwon do to improve her flexibility and balance. However, Joyce, who is now nearly eighty, healthy, and active, likes to be waited on, and sometimes she tries to use her age as an excuse to get her daughter to perform a service for her. One evening when Joyce and Roberta were planning to meet at a restaurant, Joyce called and asked her daughter to pick her up.

"I'm leaving from the office," Roberta said. "It will take

me an extra half hour to come by your house. Can't you take a taxi?"

Roberta says that her mother started to make noises about how their roles had reversed. "I told her to stop right there," Joyce says. " 'You're my mother; I'm your daughter,' I told her. 'If one day you become demented or unable to walk, I will be delighted to pick you up or take care of you, but I still won't become your mother.' "

Most experts on aging agree with Roberta. As Rose Dobrof of the Brookdale Center on Aging explains, "The idea that you become your mother's mother denies the whole history of the relationship. It denies the age of the parent, it denies what must be a key role in the life of the parent, and it robs the daughter of the experience of being an adult child."[1]

Joyce's remark was probably a shorthand way of telling Roberta that she wanted some nurturing. At any age, we can miss and long for the sense of being cosseted by a mother. But if Roberta actually *had* acted like a mother and, for example, told Joyce what to do the way a mother would with an underage child, Joyce almost certainly would have considered Roberta's behavior inappropriate.

What if a mother is mentally and physically as helpless as a baby? *Then* does she become her daughter's child? The answer is still no. A helpless mother remains a mother.

That wasn't Jane's opinion. Her mother, Tania, a writer and the widow of an international businessman, had been exceptionally independent, even after her husband died. She traveled on her own, had an apartment in London, where many of her friends—but not her daughter—

91

lived, and when she came to New York, had such an interesting circle that Jane looked forward to her mother's visits because she always met such interesting people.

Then Tania developed Alzheimer's disease. Jane had to move her into a nursing home, and her once-fascinating mother now spends most of her days in front of the television set, understanding only some of what she is watching.

"I had to sell my mother's apartment. I'm responsible for keeping track of her finances and medical insurance. I chose the home, I moved her there, and I oversee her care," Jane says. "Isn't that like being a mother?" Her voice sharpens with anger at the suggestion that her responsibilities to Tania, which now occupy a substantial portion of her time and emotional energy, are not maternal.

Yet if Jane's husband had a stroke and she were as responsible for his well-being as she is for Tania's, would she insist that she is now *his* mother? If her sister were to develop Alzheimer's and Jane had to oversee her care, would she become *her* mother? And certainly a son who was the principal caretaker and emotional supporter of his mother would not announce that he had become his mother's "father." By overseeing their mothers' care, daughters may be nurturing, supportive, protective—all maternal traits—but this is just a stage of being a good daughter.

It is much more natural for a daughter to want her mother to remain maternal than to want to swap roles with her. Sometimes daughters still look to their mothers for advice and comfort when their mothers' powers are substantially diminished.

Sandra always counted on her mother, Roslyn, for her wisdom and experience. But when Roslyn was in the early stages of Alzheimer's disease, Sandra tried to reconcile herself to the idea that her mother was no longer mentally capable of being her sounding board and advisor.

When Sandra called her, Roslyn would ask a question, usually about her grandchildren, then listen quietly while Sandra talked. When Sandra paused, Roslyn would ask the same question again.

But one evening when Sandra's daughter, Laura, was across the country working, between her sophomore and junior years in college, Sandra called her mother. Although she was sure that what she said wouldn't sink in, she tried to get through. "Laura got picked up for drunk driving, Mother," she said.

"Did they make her spend the night in jail?" Roslyn asked.

Sandra laughed in relief at her mother's sudden clarity. "Yes, they did," she said. "Now she wants to come home. What do you think we should do?"

"Wouldn't it be better for her to stay there and take her punishment?" Roslyn said.

"That's what I was thinking, too," Sandra said.

"Aren't you glad she told you?" Roslyn said.

"Yes, I am," Sandra said. "And I'm glad I told you, too."

"Just don't say anything to your father," Roslyn said. "I'm not sure he's ready to hear that his baby went to jail."

"Mom was right about that," Sandra says sadly. "Except that by then Daddy had been dead for five years. Still, when I needed her, my mother found herself long enough to come through for me. Of course, she forgot that we'd ever had the conversation, but I did call to tell her that Laura was staying out west and doing the public works program required of those who had been convicted of driving while intoxicated."

Roslyn didn't seem to absorb that information. Perhaps she understood that the crisis was over and she didn't have to call up whatever resources she had used to bring herself into the present and provide maternal solace and advice when Sandra asked for it.

When adult children financially support their parents—who once paid all *their* expenses, gave them an allowance, sent them to college, and helped out with "extras" when they were first on their own—the parallel is so obvious that it can, in fact, make a parent feel childish and cast an adult daughter (or son) in a parentlike role. This *is* a reversal of a sort, and perhaps that's one reason that the financial disparity between adult children who are earning money and parents who need their help can cause severe disruptions in the parent-child relationship. A daughter who is partly or principally supporting her parents may, in many ways, be the acting head of the family, but she is still *not* her mother's mother, and her financial generosity will be easier for her mother to accept if the daughter doesn't act as though roles that can never really be reversed have now been swapped.

Why is the mother-daughter relationship susceptible to being seen as a role reversal when the mother becomes the weaker member of the pair, even though other relationships in which one person takes the responsibility are never described in the same way? Perhaps it is because our mothers showed us what mothering looked like when we were children, and as adults we often use their nurturing style on others. When a daughter treats her mother in ways that echo how her mother once acted toward her, she may begin to feel that they have switched roles. Then the idea that a daughter has become her mother's mother drops into place, another of those orderly constructions that protects us from being swamped by the complications of untidy feelings.

In one kind of situation, the daughter does mother her mother, and that is when the nature of their relationship has always been unbalanced. Some mothers are not physically or emotionally strong enough to act in a motherly way and, as soon as they can, begin to train their daughters to take care of them or to become "little mothers" to their younger siblings. This is a particularly poisonous example of what has been described as "the tyranny of the weak." Children of alcoholics are a subset: forced to take care of a mother who has passed out or who can't walk upstairs on her own, they quite rightly feel that they are playing the maternal role.

Most mothers and daughters do not swap places, yet the balance does shift. Part of the adjustment is for daughters to recognize their responsibility to handle change with respect, to care for their mothers when appropriate and without bullying, and to resist allowing their mothers to use "role reversal" as an excuse to lean on their daughters when they would remain strong longer by standing on their own.

CHAPTER 8

⁓

The "Good Enough" Daughter

Being Responsible

The idea of the "good enough" daughter, who does her best and can forgive herself for her imperfections, is one that a "good enough" mother would understand. Whether or not a mother accepts a daughter's best (yet not faultless) efforts, a woman who wishes to be a good daughter to her aging mother tries to achieve three qualities. The first is to be responsible, the second is to be companionable, and the third is to be loving.

No matter how much you love your mother, if you are not available when she really needs you, you have let her down. A mother and daughter may have quite different ideas of what "need" really means. In *Helping Elderly Parents: The Role of Adult Children*, Victor G. Cicirelli, whose specialty is developmental and aging psychology, reported that researchers found that parents and children don't always agree about priorities. While parents are concerned with crime and safety, government and business red tape, and even "with a need to have sufficient reading material to maintain realistic contact with the world," Cicirelli writes, their adult children tend to focus more on "home health care and personal care," which the parents worry about less.[1]

By not asking them, daughters miss the chance to find out what their mothers feel they need. While some mothers are so demanding that their daughters can't avoid knowing exactly what they want, others—mine among them—are considerably less forthcoming and ask for as little as possible. Recently, I inquired of my mother how she felt about looking older. "It doesn't bother me particularly," she said. (That's probably because Mother has always been beautiful, and she still is.) But then I asked her what *does* bother her now. "I don't like being alone," she said.

If I had been just guessing, I might have picked something else, for example, cooking for herself, which I know Mother doesn't enjoy. But I *did* ask, and it clarified something I hadn't quite realized: Mother would prefer it if I stopped by more often, perhaps just for a half hour while I'm walking my dog, rather than if I brought the ingredients, cooked her dinner, and stayed longer but did it less frequently.

Whatever else a mother needs from a responsible daughter, she usually would like to know how to reach her and to feel that her daughter is keeping track of her as well.

Mary Anne, an only child who lives near her mother, Abby, but sees her only a couple of times a month and calls about three times a week, says that when she is going out of town on business, even if it's only for a short time, her mother gets anxious. "What if something happens to me?" Abby asks.

"I'll leave you the number where I'm staying and you'll call me," Mary Anne says. "If it's serious, I'll come home. If it isn't, we'll talk about it. If you lose my number, you can always call my assistant." Abby has never had to call Mary Anne when she's away, but they both feel more comfortable because they know that Mary Anne is not entirely out of contact.

Mary Anne has taken other steps to be sure Abby can get help if something goes wrong. After Abby fell a couple of times when she got up to go to the bathroom in the middle of the night, Mary Anne found out where her mother could buy an emergency beeper that she can wear around her neck. She gave her the literature, and Abby ordered the equipment. Now Abby feels less exposed, even when her daughter is out of town.

Mary Anne has also made a point of getting to know the woman who lives next door to her mother in her apartment building. "Luckily, Mother's neighbor is very nice," Mary Anne says. "I asked her if I could call her in an emergency, and she said of course. I keep her phone number and the building number with me wherever I go. Mother knows I can check up on her if she doesn't answer her phone at a time when she wouldn't be out—early in the morning, for example, or when the weather is terrible. I think it makes her feel as though I'm watching out for her, and it certainly makes me more comfortable."

Many daughters take on tasks that are easier for them than for their mothers or that might not get done at all if a daughter didn't do them. Often daughters who are more accustomed to dealing with paperwork fill in their mothers' Medicare, tax, and insurance forms. Some shop for food to be sure their mothers eat well. One walks her mother's dog when the weather is bad and her mother can't get out of her apartment. The dog, a miniature poodle, is paper-trained, but its mistress feels guilty when it is confined to the house without exercise or diversion all day. Many daughters accompany their mothers to doctors' and dentists' appointments and, if their mothers agree, sit in on their conferences with the doctors.

Some, who are too busy or live too far away to do these tasks themselves find and arrange for local elder assistance groups to stand in for them, providing services that are either free or low-cost. I recently learned that my mother paid an accountant nearly as much as he recovered for her in a health insurance mixup that was caused when a doctor charged her double for a minor operation. Mother, like many older women without much business experience, was taken advantage of twice: first by the doctor, then by the accountant. I mentioned this to a friend who is on the board of the Burden Center for the Aging, and she told me that a volunteer could have handled this situation for free—and because the center specializes in helping older people, probably faster and more effectively. To be honest, if Mother had asked me to take on that project, I not only wouldn't have had the time, but I would have been as confused as she was by how to go about it. That's a case where a good daughter would have figured out how to call in assistance.

Being responsible can mean taking on a serious situation a mother can't handle or doesn't want to face, even though a daughter's "interference" might make her mother angry.

Clara, a retired schoolteacher, lived on her own until she was in her early nineties. Clara had always been self-sufficient. She had never had many friends and was happy to spend her days reading and keeping her small apartment tidy. She cooked for herself, ate light, healthy meals, and seemed to need very little company, aside from her eighteen-year-old cat. Her daughter, Stephanie, who lived a couple of hours away, spent one weekend a month with her, but Clara's apartment was so small that Stephanie had the impression that her mother was just as glad when Stephanie left and she had her little world to herself again.

Then Clara's cat died. Less than a month later, when Stephanie went to visit her mother, the apartment seemed dusty, and the refrigerator was emptier than usual. On her next visit, Stephanie could see that Clara's disintegration had become quite severe. She had stopped bathing, washing her hair, and cleaning her apartment, and she had virtually stopped eating.

Clara had lost so much weight that Stephanie suggested she consult with a doctor at the local hospital who specialized in geriatric health. Clara agreed, so Stephanie made an appointment for her and arranged for a neighbor to drive her there. But after the appointment, when Stephanie called to ask her what the doctor said, Clara couldn't remember. Finally, Stephanie called the doctor herself. He told her that Clara was suffering from malnutrition.

The doctor recommended an eldercare aide, who, for a small fee, would come in for an hour a day and make lunch for Clara. But after a couple of weeks, the aide called Stephanie and said that her mother wouldn't get out of bed, that the sheets hadn't been changed for weeks, and that the aide was taking out the garbage because Clara wouldn't do it herself.

"The next time I went to see Mother, I told her that it seemed as though the time had come for her to move into a elder community with full health, meal, and housekeeping services. Mother didn't want to move, but I couldn't responsibly leave her to live that way.

"I found a place that sounded promising, spent most of a day there, and liked it. Mother could afford the reasonable cost, and it was close enough so I could still see her regularly. The staff was pleasant, the residents were dressed and clean, and there was plenty to do. There was a kind of upbeat spirit; the noise level in the dining room seemed just right, not too quiet, as though people had a lot to say to each other. The apartments were small, but so was the apartment Mother had been living in for the last twenty years."

Stephanie told her mother that she had arranged for her to move. Clara was upset and resistant, but although she didn't want to visit the community, she didn't refuse to live there. Stephanie took a week's leave from her job, rented a room in a bed-and-breakfast—by this time, her mother's apartment was barely habitable—and went over each day to pack whatever she could salvage. Some of Clara's clothes and furniture were so dirty and tattered that they had to go to the town dump. Through all this, Clara stayed in bed and watched. "Mother looked at me as though I was murdering her. But the truth is that the way she was living, she was committing slow suicide," Stephanie says.

Despite her unwillingness to move, once Clara arrived at her new home, she settled in quickly. "Mother found a man who was looking for a chess partner," Stephanie reports. "She had always wanted to learn to play chess, but she'd never gotten around to it. Now he has taught her, and the two of them sit over the chessboard for hours. She still likes to be 'quiet,' as she calls it, so she often eats alone, but since the home brings meals to the residents' rooms, she is getting three meals a day. Mother seems happier than she has for years, but even if she *didn't* like it there, as long as she is treated well, she is much better off than the way she was when she was living by herself, mourning her cat," Stephanie says.

It is not always clear when a mother's quality of life has diminished past the point where it is safe and healthy for her to continue living on her own. (If a daughter considers the way her mother lives to be "unacceptable," it is useful to remember that housekeeping standards aren't absolute.) Sometimes it makes sense to call in an objective observer—as Stephanie did with the doctor and the eldercare aide—to be sure a daughter isn't overreacting to conditions that, while hardly optimal, don't warrant interference.

When it is evident that a mother's life has spun out of control, as Clara's did, her daughter may have to brave her mother's anger and resistance and make tough decisions. Her mother may feel sad that she has lost the life she once led, but when a daughter is really justified in stepping in, her mother has already stopped leading that life.

And when a daughter acts out of love and concern and makes responsible choices, her mother's dismay at the changes her daughter insists on can be balanced by her satisfaction that her daughter cares enough to spend the time and attention to assure that she is taken care of.

Even if a mother complains and resists, certain situations are not ambiguous. That was the case when my mother-in-law began to develop dementia. One afternoon, she got in her car and drove aimlessly until she ran out of gas. She lived on Long Island, and late that night, when she'd run through a full tank, she came to a stop in Brooklyn. No one knows how long she sat, alone and confused, in her car before the police, who had been alerted to look for an Oldsmobile with her license plate, found her and brought her home. After that, my brother-in-law took away her car keys. But because she couldn't remember why she wasn't allowed to drive anymore, my mother-in-law would berate the nurse who was on duty for "bossing her around." My brother-in-law left a letter for the nurses to show her, in which he explained why she couldn't drive and that the decision was his, not a nurse's. Of course, my mother-in-law then denounced her extremely dutiful and loving son as "bossy," too.

On the scale of complexity in the relationship between parents and adult children, certainly a high rating goes to situations in which a daughter (or in the case of my mother-in-law, who didn't have any daughters, a son) takes charge and overrules her mother's wishes. The mother may become angry and stay that way. Her anger may serve to distract her from frustration at her impotence in the face of the ticking clock and a failing body. Even when a daughter is clearly right, she may feel guilty that she has the power to force her mother to do something she doesn't want to do.

Other situations that require responsible intervention can come up quite unexpectedly. Among them are problems with alcohol and prescription drugs that were never issues before. Suddenly, the body's declining ability to metabolize alcohol—or the interaction of liquor and new medications—can turn a moderate social drinker into a person with a "drinking problem."

At any age, people who are prescribed drugs to manage pain can become addicted and continue to take them long after the pain is gone. Drug abuse is usually a problem to be handled with the help of a doctor, but when drinking gets out of hand, the person who has to take the responsibility to intervene is often a daughter. And a woman who has enjoyed social drinking may feel that changing her habits is an unwelcome sign that age has robbed her of yet another pleasure.

Maggie and Lindsay are sisters. Their mother, Marjorie, had always had what she describes as "a drink and a dividend" before dinner, without adverse effects. Then, as she reached her late seventies, Marjorie's capacity for alcohol diminished. Marjorie began to slur her words halfway through the first drink, which both annoyed and embarrassed her daughters. As for talking on the phone, by the time her daughters got home from work and called her, Marjorie could often barely enunciate.

What really worried Maggie and Lindsay was that Marjorie wasn't very steady on her feet anymore, even when she *hadn't* been drinking. They were sure that it was just a matter of time before she fell and hurt herself. "She doesn't think about what will happen if she breaks her hip," Lindsay said, "and guess who's going to have to take care of her."

The sisters began their assault on Marjorie's drinking at a bad time: they were at a restaurant, the waiter was standing by, and Marjorie ordered her usual vodka on the rocks. Lindsay suggested that she have a glass of wine instead. Marjorie was upset; she refused to change her order, and the atmosphere was tense for the rest of the meal. On a couple of other occasions, Lindsay and Maggie tried to convince their mother to reconsider her drinking pattern—but always just as she was either about to order a drink or to pour one for herself—and each time Marjorie was defensive and stubborn.

Finally, one night Marjorie fell on the path outside a friend's house when she was leaving after dinner. She got a bump on the back of her head and was shaken up for a couple of days. Maggie and Lindsay decided to use the accident as a wedge. They made a date to go to their mother's house—before the cocktail hour—to have a serious talk with her.

They told her that it was evident that her ability to metabolize alcohol had diminished and that they had come to ask her to cut down on her drinking. Marjorie bristled, said they were "spoiling her fun," and insisted, "I'm not drinking any more than I ever did."

"Yes, but you weighed twenty pounds more when you were sixty than you do now," Lindsay said. "And you weren't taking all these medications you're on."

"Well, I'll see," Marjorie said.

"That's up to you, Mother," Maggie said, "but neither of us will go out to dinner with you again if you drink more than a glass of wine."

Marjorie found a way to save face and take over the situation. She told her daughters she would ask her doctor if there was any interaction between her medications and liquor. She did, and he advised her not to drink more than one jigger of vodka a day, and to stick with a single glass of wine when she went out. Marjorie has followed his advice—most of the time—and Maggie and Lindsay enjoy her company again and see her more often.

While a mother may take the view that a responsible daughter will help her with errands and paperwork and be easy to reach in an emergency—assistance that doesn't involve "interference"—in situations that compromise health and safety, a daughter must take a more active role. If her mother resists, the daughter can remind herself of the old maternal saying "You'll thank me later"—just as long as she doesn't say it out loud. I doubt a mother would be any more pleased to hear it than her daughter once was.

Companionship and Love

If the first quality a mother hopes for in her daughter is that she be responsible, the second is that she provide attention and companionship. The anthropologist Helen E. Fisher, speaking of her mother's final illness, comments, "When the rest of the world shuts down for mothers, more and more, they make connections to their daughters. But daughters are still out there making new connections for their own survival. It was an imbalance that I could not win. My mother couldn't win, either. Every time I gave everything I could, she wanted more."[2]

Being companionable, rather than just dutiful, can require ingenuity.

Elaina's mother, Katherine, was housebound for a couple of months while she was recovering from pneumonia. With little outside stimulation, she didn't have much to talk about except her health when Elaina came to see her. Then Elaina found a way to make their visits fun and interesting for both of them.

Elaina reviews movies for a weekly newspaper, and one evening she brought the tape of a movie she was writing about to Katherine's house. They had a simple dinner, which Elaina cooked, and then they watched the movie. Neither of them could quite decide whether they liked it, and, in explaining to Katherine what the press materials said the director was getting at, Elaina clarified her own opinion. Katherine called her a couple of times over the next few days to discuss the movie further. They both enjoyed the whole process so much that, even when she didn't have a film to review, Elaina began stopping by the video rental store and picking up a couple of videotapes for her mother to choose between so they could watch one of them together.

Katherine is fully recovered, but the video evenings have continued. "It gives us a lot to talk about," Elaina says. "Not just the movies, but themes the plots bring up."

When visiting isn't possible, other forms of attention can be almost as satisfying. Christine Cassell of the Mount Sinai Medical Center, whose mother has since died, says, "I remember once calling from Chicago to a pizza place in a suburb of Boston, where my mother lived, to have pizza delivered to her house because I knew she was sitting there, not eating anything."[3]

Sometimes a problem crops up that could cause a rift that will interfere with a mother and daughter's companionship. It often falls on the daughter to force herself not to turn her back when something happens that causes her mother to behave badly.

Fay had just arrived at her mother's house, where Fay and her husband planned to spend a summer weekend. Her mother, Carolyn, was out, so when the phone rang Fay answered. The caller was her brother, who had been a paraplegic since a car accident a couple of years earlier.

"I just spoke to Mom and she told me to call and tell you that she wants you out of the house before she gets there," he said.

"What!" Fay said. "What have I done?"

"Search me," her brother said, "but I'd get out of there if I were you."

Fay and her husband were discussing what to do when Carolyn drove up and got out of the car.

"Mom! What's wrong?" Fay asked.

Carolyn, who is usually quite controlled, had tears rolling down her cheeks, and Fay said, "Sorry, Mom, we're not going anywhere until you tell us what happened."

Carolyn confessed that she didn't want anyone to see how upset she was. The reason: her son had just told her that traveling had become so difficult that he wouldn't be coming to stay with Carolyn that summer.

Carolyn could hardly vent her disappointment on her son, so she turned on her daughter. Although Fay was hurt and confused, she stuck around and worked it out with her mother, and Carolyn, who particularly needed her daughter's company that weekend, didn't have to spend it alone.

That was an isolated incident, and it wasn't typical of Carolyn's behavior. When she and Fay had sorted things out, they were able to return to their long-standing pattern of friendship. But some mothers are consistently irrational or unpleasant, and it's not uncommon for people to get worse with age. It can be extremely difficult to be a companionable daughter to a disagreeable mother, but many women try.

Betsy takes her mother, Lydia, to a restaurant for dinner once a week. Lydia, now in her late eighties, has always had a sharp tongue, and Betsy, the youngest of three children, has developed a protective mechanism: when Lydia is unpleasant, Betsy just pretends she hasn't spoken.

One evening while Betsy and Lydia were having dinner, Betsy mentioned that she had made a reservation for the following Sunday night at a new Japanese restaurant. Lydia's reaction was typical. She glowered and said, "I don't have any appetite. I don't know why you waste your money. I'd just as soon stay home."

As usual, Betsy ignored her mother's comments and changed the subject. Then Lydia simmered and waited for the chance to strike again. When Betsy got home, she took a couple of antacid pills, as she often does after a meal with her mother.

Betsy's daughter, Gail, in her late twenties, sometimes joined her mother and grandmother on their restaurant nights. Betsy noticed that Gail, who is less emotionally tangled up with her grandmother, was able to defuse Lydia when she started on her usual tirade.

"My eyes were really opened one night when Gail was there," Betsy says. "Mother went on about not being hungry and so on, and Gail told her the point of the dinners was more so Mother and I could have the pleasure of seeing each other than what or where we ate. Gail said, 'If you don't enjoy eating out that much, why don't you and Mom go to the movies together in the afternoon and then go out for tea?'

"I was reacting to my mother's tone of voice, which

has always been so critical. Gail was listening to what she said," Betsy comments. "Gail realized that Mother wasn't just being difficult; she really doesn't like eating a big meal. We tried the movies and tea routine, and while I'm not saying that Mother has suddenly become sweet, it was much pleasanter. Now we only have dinner out once in a while, but we still see each other every week."

Women like Lydia who seem barely able to suppress their anger may be naturally crabby, but they may also be in pain or raging at their frailty or at the knowledge that they can't look ahead to more than a few more years of life. They unload their anger on the person most likely to stick around and take it—who is usually a daughter. Sometimes a daughter can alleviate her mother's rage; sometimes she can't. One woman whose mother complained bitterly and incessantly tried a technique that had worked with her son when he was a little boy. At night, when she put him to bed, he would say, "This was not my lucky day," and then recite his grievances. After a while, his mother, who was worried that he had a disturbingly negative view of his life, proposed the following compromise: "You can tell me three bad things that happened to you today," she said, "but then you have to tell me three good things." He rose to the challenge. Her mother did, too.

But whether a mother is a pleasure to be with or a bundle of complaints and criticisms, most daughters find a way to take some responsibility and provide some companionship. It is just too difficult to forgive yourself for walking away from the longest relationship of your life.

Responsibility and companionship are critical aspects of being a good daughter, but, of course, the underlying and

110

immeasurably important ingredient is love. While love can't be manufactured, the soil in which it grows can be fertilized. It is easier to be a loving daughter if you have a clear conscience—and being dutiful and companionable are excellent remedies for guilt. Even so, the old patterns—both those shared by mothers and daughters from one era to the next and those that spike each relationship—can continue to interfere with their ability to express, and sometimes feel, the love they know is there. That's when a daughter may have to accept her limitations, keep trying anyway, and allow herself to be a "good enough" daughter who does the best she can and who hopes that her mother can love her the way we all want to be loved—despite our failings and not just because of our successes.

"I don't feel old."

Sarinda Dranow, 1998. Mother, at eighty, still worked two days a week as a hospital volunteer. When people meet her, they invariably comment on her beauty. *Photograph by Ellen Warner.*

PART II

Profiles

CHAPTER 9

~

Real Lives

Up to now, I have focused on the way changes in the culture have affected family relationships; on the innate push and pull of the mother-daughter bond, which has *not* changed; on the reality of being old in our society; and on the new role daughters formulate as our mothers age. That role, as I have said, is not to become our mothers' mothers. It is to be daughters who have to juggle different kinds of responsibilities than women had when our mothers faced our grandmothers' aging, while preparing ourselves to become the older generation when our mothers die. Those are the baselines we share.

Understanding that we are not alone, and how outside forces influence us, relieves some of the pressure we put on ourselves, and calms the internal critic whose partner is guilt. But within that general context is the personal, and singular: the way each particular mother ages, and the way each mother and daughter feel about each other. No matter how many others are in the "sandwich generation," the variations on the sandwich menu are infinite.

Through the profiles of daughters in this section I have explored how commonly shared situations play out in particular relationships. By going back to their early interactions, I have sought to find out why, as their mothers age, daughters react as they do. Hearing the scenarios one sometimes feels like a member of the audience at a movie, trying not to scream, "Look out behind you!" because in back of each woman is a long history that waits in the shadows with a blunt or sharp instrument to wound her. When we hear that one woman's mother was so negligent that she didn't attend her daughter's high school graduation, it makes sense that even in her forties, that daughter is still trying to get her mother's attention; and that, hoping for approval, she can't say no to her unreasonable demands. We want to call out, "Stop! You've done enough! You *are* a good daughter; you don't have to be a martyr." That woman, like the other daughters who told me their stories, may not have been able to overcome the deep feelings that tripped her up, but she spoke to me because she hoped that others would learn from her.

I have not tried to set up stories as representative of types, but I have juxtaposed those with common denominators. Some profiles are organized according to an external circumstance, for example to show the way different mothers and daughters cope with such similar situations as living thousands of miles apart. But within each of these stories are other, dissimilar elements. Like life, these stories resist classification, yet all of them have qualities that resonate with many mother-daughter relationships.

It is always easier to be objective about someone else's life. I found that hearing other women's stories helped me sort out what is—and isn't—important in my own. The small, petty irritations can be the hardest to handle graciously, and when I noticed how common mother-daughter hair stories were, I realized I could catch myself when I began to bristle in anticipation of my mother's critique of my current haircut or color. (Then, after she read the manuscript of this book, my mother stopped mentioning my hair at all. Some things *can* change.)

Most significant, though, especially when I heard the longing in the voices of women who had the most difficult relationships with their mothers, I understood how crucial it is for a daughter to find a way to go through the end of life in step with her mother. A sense of duty certainly is one reason that daughters make disruptive life choices to help their aging mothers—quitting their jobs, moving, driving a couple of hours each way to spend sparse leisure time with them. But of all the insights I took away from these stories, told by women who sometimes laughed at themselves, occasionally burst out in anger, and often had tears in their eyes, the one that comes through most clearly is this: daughters instinctively understand that, if a torch is to be passed, the runners must be in stride.

The women in these profiles try their best to be good daughters, even when they don't have much control over such intractable circumstances as health, finances, their mothers' personalities, and just plain luck. Perfection generally eludes them, but, although they may never be convinced that it is true, their best is usually good enough.

CHAPTER 10

❧

Making Decisions Together

Assisted Living

Where a mother should live when she is failing but not severely disabled is one of the gray areas of aging. Often an
older person *can* live on her own, but at a certain point—
perhaps after a household accident or when a lingering
cold has kept her home and isolated for weeks—her adult
children begin to wonder if it is time for her to exchange
the advantages of independence for the benefits of communal living. If a daughter thinks her mother is not quite
up to living alone and her mother is determined to stay
where she is, the conflict can bring out old resentments
and anger.

It can be hard to keep in mind that what seems like the
perfect solution to a daughter may feel more like the final
solution to her mother. Often the mother's interests and
the daughter's are at odds; sometimes they simply bring
different perspectives to the situation.

While a mother worries about losing her independence,
her daughter may be afraid that, if her mother continues
to live on her own, she will become so dependent that she

will compromise her daughter's autonomy. A daughter may want to hand over more responsibility to an eldercare community; her mother would rather risk falling down the stairs and breaking her leg in her own house than move to a place designed for maximum safety but which she is sure will never feel like home.

Communal living is often much less familiar to women of our mother's generation than to those of us who went to camp or college. For the girl who won the prizes at camp, living with others may feel like a return to a happy time; for the one who sat in the corner of her bunk, reading and crossing off the days on her calendar until she could go home, it can seem like prison; and for a woman who has never lived under the same roof with anyone she wasn't related to, it can threaten a permanent absence of privacy.

Money is an issue, too: when the entry fee to an assisted-living community is not refundable and can be as high as hundreds of thousands of dollars, both mothers and daughters worry that the depletion of capital will strip the mother's estate and deprive her daughter of an inheritance that could have helped the daughter in *her* old age. Even a mother who would prefer to move may decide not to do so because she is saving her money to leave something behind that will protect her daughter.

Moving is always difficult, often more so for people as they age. Every "stress list" includes moving, even to a bigger and better house. Add to that stress the fear that the next resting place after assisted living is either a nursing home or the grave, and it is hardly surprising that many older people prefer to stay where they are.

Considering the innately disturbing prospect of moving—both away from a longtime home and into a situation that has overtones of intrusion, loss, and finality—it is not surprising that the prospect of change can stir up a mess of emotions in both mother and daughter. That's what happened to Lucy and her mother, Alice, when Lucy decided that her parents should leave their dream house and move into a nearby assisted-living complex.

⁓

LUCY AND ALICE

"It's not a nursing home; it's more like a luxury hotel."

It is Thanksgiving Day, and Lucy's family has gathered at her house—white, clapboard, colonial—on the eastern shore of Maryland. Outside the dining room windows, the lawn, now covered with a light fur of snow, slopes down to the bay, where a glittering pink stripe on the water reflects the last of the November sun. The house is filled with early American furniture and folk art, rag rugs, and old hand-forged tools to tend the fires in the three downstairs fireplaces. It should be a perfect setting for Thanksgiving—but houses are inhabited by people, who, especially on holidays, often manage to impose their own moods on even the most ideal surroundings.

Lucy and a friend are at the sink in the kitchen, scraping leftovers off the dishes from the main course before they bring out the pumpkin and apple pies. Lucy lowers her voice so she can't be heard in the dining room and says, "I can't believe my mother did that."

"I'll bet women in kitchens all over America are muttering, 'Did you hear what my mother just said?' " the friend responds, and the two women look at each other and laugh.

Just before the table was cleared, Lucy had stood up with an old clothbound book in her hand. In preparation for the holiday, she had gone to the library and found a local history with a couple of pages about her ancestors, who were among the first settlers in this town where Lucy's parents and sister and brother-in-law still live. Lucy and her husband, Mark, who work in Baltimore, spend weekends there.

Lucy had read a couple of paragraphs when her mother, Alice, interrupted her. "You think you know so much about our family," Alice said. "Well, I'll bet you didn't know that your great-great-uncle George was a forger and went to jail."

"No, I didn't know," Lucy said, almost patiently. "Would you like to hear the rest?" The others at the table nodded. Lucy's father, Daniel, who is eighty-four and quite deaf, missed most of the interchange, but he kept smiling as Alice, undeterred, kept talking about the felonious George. "Well," Lucy said, putting the book down. "It's all here if the rest of you want to take a look after dinner. I'm going to bring in the dessert."

In the kitchen, Lucy sighs. "My mother has always been competitive with me," she says. "And it's gotten worse lately. You know she was really beautiful until a couple of years ago, but since she's started to look old, her favorite subject is how much better she held up when she was my age than I have. She says things like, 'I never got those jowls,' and then she points to my chin. Sometimes she pinches me to see if I have any extra weight around the middle. I guess she's jealous."

Then Lucy and her friend each pick up a pie and go back into the dining room. It is dark outside now, and Lucy lights the candles, while Mark opens a bottle of champagne and toasts their family. When Lucy looks at Alice, she sees that her mother's eyes are filling with tears, and she reaches over and touches her hand.

"Each year I wonder how many times we'll all be together again," Alice says. "This is very nice, dear."

But by the end of the afternoon, Lucy and Alice pick up what has become their most urgent subject of conversation, and the mood changes again, as it so often does—another echo of the push and pull that underlies mother-daughter relationships. Lucy is convinced that it is no longer safe or stimulating for Alice and Daniel to stay in their home; she wants them to move into an assisted-living facility nearby. Although Daniel is willing to go, Alice is fighting to stay in her house, with the garden she started thirty years ago.

Later, Lucy says, "I don't even want to think about what's going on with my parents." In fact, she thinks about it all the time.

"My mother grew up in this town," Lucy says. "She lived next door to her grandparents when she was a child and came back after a year of college to marry my father. *He* grew up here, too." Alice and Daniel hadn't been married for long when Alice's grandparents died and left their house to her, and she and Daniel moved in. When Alice was making breakfast, she could look out her kitchen window and see her mother in *her* kitchen, across the yard.

Alice was twenty-four when Lucy was born; she had Lucy's sister, Joan, a couple of years later. Like most middle-class women of her generation, Alice didn't work outside the house, but she was also agoraphobic, frightened to drive any farther than the town limits. She has still never been on an airplane, and, at eighty, she is likely to live out her life without flying.

When Alice was in her fifties, her parents died. With the small legacy they left her, she and Daniel were able to buy what Lucy calls their dream house—same town, better neighborhood. "That's the house where they live now," Lucy says.

Although Daniel had a steady job, he never earned a lot of money. When he retired with a small pension and Social Security, Lucy, who is a trial lawyer, and Mark, a successful investment banker, became Lucy's parents' principal source of support. Since Alice and Daniel have become financially dependent on their daughter, when Alice disagrees with Lucy, her resistance is often subversive rather than direct—like her hostile interruption at Thanksgiving dinner.

Lucy hoped that, with the security she and Mark provided for them, her parents might travel and enjoy their older years. But she says, "My mother has become even less adventuresome. Now she doesn't leave the house without my father."

Alice's territory was always limited, but now she has stopped driving entirely, and a series of illnesses, including a couple of minor strokes, have left her frail, so she is nearly housebound. "I don't think my parents go out more than a couple of times a week," Lucy says. "They seem so isolated. Even though my sister lives only a half hour away, she works full-time and she has small children at home. So she can't get over to see them as much as she'd like to, either.

"My parents don't have a large group of acquaintances," Lucy continues, "but they used to be outgoing and sociable within their own circle. They ran an amateur choral group until a few years ago; my mother sang and my father conducted. They can't do that anymore, so they started volunteering at the thrift shop for a homeless shelter. But the younger volunteers haven't been very nice; they act like they're doing them a favor to let them come. It breaks my heart to see my parents now; they used to have so much fun together.

"It's not really safe for them to live alone, either. This is the kind of thing that happens: my parents have a dog, and the other day the dog threw up, and my mother slipped on its vomit and fell and cut her head. She called for my father, but since he's practically deaf and he hates to wear his hearing aid, he didn't hear her." She grimaces. "Who knows what will be next?

"So I'm thinking that my parents could enjoy themselves in the assisted-living place and make new friends— *and* I wouldn't have to worry about their safety."

Lucy found out that a partial-care community was about to open a couple of towns away. She thought it sounded as though it would suit her parents very well and told her mother about its many advantages: the dining room and pub, the beauty parlor, the van to take them shopping or to a movie or concert, the nurses on duty.

Alice listened and shook her head. "I don't want to go to a nursing home," she said.

Lucy tried again. "It's not a nursing home. It's more like a luxury hotel," she said. But Alice was never interested in even the best hotels; she just likes her home.

Lucy worries about Alice, and Alice worries about her. "My mother is very, very neurotic," Lucy says. "If I go on an airplane trip, she's capable of calling me the day before and saying she heard there was going to be a thunderstorm. And then *I* start to fret. My mother has an uncanny ability to invoke my anxieties. Sometimes I do the same kind of thing to my daughters." Even though both daughters are over thirty, Lucy is apt to remind one of them to be sure to take a taxi if she's going to be out late at night or to send the other a new nutrition supplement because she thinks she's missing meals.

"The one thing my mother *didn't* worry about," Lucy says, "is her old age. I'm angry that she didn't make a plan for herself—that she didn't *grow up* and make a plan for herself—and now I have to do it. This is how 'out of it' my mother is about money. My father was sick last winter, so we had a visiting nurse come once a week. My mother wanted to know if she could come more often, but the nurse said, 'I can't do that unless you're a charity case. I'd have to see your finances.' So my mother showed her their tax return, and it turns out they qualify. At first my mother was horrified, but then she told me, 'Since I'm a charity, you could give me money and deduct it as a charitable contribution.' I hate to think what she's going to do if my father dies first."

Lucy and Joan agreed to provide services for their parents at home on a trial basis to see if they could accommodate Alice's wish to stay in her house. They hired a health-care aide, but Alice considers her presence an intrusion, and with Daniel's passive cooperation, she is doing her best to cut back on her hours. "The health-care aide is supposed to work from nine to six, but on her first day, my mother told her she didn't have to come in until ten; around four in the afternoon, she insists that she go home," Lucy says. "They can't wait to get her out of their house. They only consented to have her at all because my mother thinks it will stall their move to assisted living.

"When we got the aide, my mother had to fire the cleaning lady—who didn't clean and who showed up whenever she felt like it; my mother was incapable of pinning her down to a schedule. So my mother wrote the cleaning lady a letter and asked me to give it to her because she also works for one of my neighbors. My mother left the envelope open—she said I was supposed to fill in something, but, of course, she wanted me to read the letter. In it she said she hoped the cleaning lady understood, but her daughters—her big, bad daughters—were forcing her to do this, and that was the price she had to pay to stay in her own home."

Alice and Daniel recently confessed that the aide has been disagreeable. "To tell you the truth, we're afraid of her," Daniel told Lucy. Alice elaborated: "The other day I wanted to take a nap, but she was sitting on my bed watching television," Alice said. "I told her I'd like to lie down. 'Go ahead,' she said. 'You won't disturb me.' "

"And she just sat there on your bed with the TV on?" Lucy asked.

"Well, yes," Alice said.

"Why didn't you tell her to go downstairs to her own room and watch television there?" Lucy asked.

"How do you tell someone to get off your bed if she doesn't think of it herself?" Alice said. Once she'd gotten up the nerve to report on the aide's bad behavior, she reported a list of similar offenses.

"So we'll find someone else," Lucy said. Later, she admitted that she was sure her parents had been reluctant to complain because they were afraid if they didn't accept whomever Lucy hired, she would put more pressure on them to move out of their house.

"I had heard about what's called 'elder abuse,' " Lucy says. "I'd even seen public service ads about it. But I thought that was the sort of thing that happened in really bad nursing homes. If you're hiring someone to take care of a child who is too young to talk or who is afraid to tell her parents when the nanny is mean, you find ways to check up on the caretaker. I realized that my parents are at the mercy of whoever is working for them, too. I'm going to be much more careful about who I hire the next time. But, to be honest, this is just another example of why my parents would be better off in a well-run assisted-living community."

Lucy understands that her financial power is one reason that Alice takes a circuitous route when she tries to undermine her daughter's decisions. But Lucy says, "I'm tired of my mother's guerrilla tactics. Basically, I don't want to deal with her about this anymore. I hired a geriatric social worker, who came to my office and spent an hour with me, talking about how to persuade my parents to move. I intend to force the issue. I haven't told my parents yet, but I've already put down the deposit on the place near them. One way or another, I'm going to get this whole thing solved."

A few months later, when the assisted-living community opened, Lucy and a friend drove over for a tour. The apartments were small and characterless, the public rooms looked as though they had been planned by the designer of an upscale motel, there were no books in the "library" and no outdoor living space, and the view from the windows was a busy road. The facility's principal advantages seemed to be that it was safe and clean and that Alice and Daniel, who often forget to eat, would have most of their meals in the dining room. By contrast, although their house is cluttered and *not* very clean, it is big and filled—crammed—with possessions and keepsakes, and they spend most of their days on a pretty, glassed-in porch overlooking the garden.

Despite the residence's lack of charm, Lucy still thought moving there was a compromise her parents should make, and she convinced them to go with her and Joan to a luncheon for prospective residents. Alice conceded that the food was good and the dining room was "nice," although she thought the plastic flowers were ugly—but she balked at looking at an apartment. Finally, she agreed but refused to take the elevator to the second floor because elevators give her claustrophobia. "I'll walk," she said and managed to trip and fall on the way up the stairs. After she'd regained her composure in the residents' lounge, Alice peered in the door of an apartment, announced that it was "much too small," and left. It was small: the downstairs of Alice and Daniel's house is considerably larger and, even though it's untidy, more attractive.

"I still think they'd be better off moving," Lucy says, "but I'm giving up. I've gotten my deposit back."

Is that the kind of setup Lucy imagines for herself when she's in her eighties? "Not really," she says, "but I don't want to be dependent on my daughters, either."

Here's what she's thinking of doing: "There's a street in Cambridge, right near Harvard Yard," she says. "I already know three families who live there. I can imagine myself retiring to a house on that block and, even if Mark dies before I do, I won't be lonely. In the mornings, my friends and I can go in and out of each other's kitchens for coffee, and we can walk to Harvard for lectures and maybe audit classes." This retirement nirvana sounds rather like a more intellectual version of her mother's small-town life—the life Alice isn't ready to sacrifice for a safer, more sterile environment.

Living with Ambiguity

How did a daughter who wants the best for her parents find herself in a situation where she can't get comfortable with their not unreasonable choices?

Anxiety is a ribbon that runs through Lucy and Alice's relationship. Alice, agoraphobic and timid, brought up a daughter who was determined not to lead as narrow a life as her mother did. Lucy is worldly, successful, and well traveled, but she hasn't fully left her mother's legacy of fearfulness behind. She responds to her fears by being annoyed with Alice for evoking them in the first place and by trying to "solve the whole thing" because she is distracted by her worries about what might happen if all the loose ends aren't tied up.

Among the techniques Lucy uses to prevent the catastrophes Alice always warned her about is to manage, organize, and reduce a situation to a series of problems and solutions (surely one reason she is a good lawyer). The assisted-living community has the appeal of containing most of the possible problems.

Lucy is trying, through her efficiency, to prove to herself that she is not like her mother and won't end up dependent on her daughters, but Lucy *is* like her mother, at least in the way she shows her love: by worrying and fussing. Ironically, Alice is actually more open to ambiguity about this part of her life than Lucy is. Despite all the things Alice is afraid of, she is brave enough to accept the consequences of maintaining her own home for as long as she can.

Lucy is also angry that her mother is so dependent—the way she has vowed never to be—but dependence is one of her mother's salient characteristics, and Lucy has some investment in her continuing to be that way. The closer we get to losing our mothers entirely, the more we are apt to cling to even their least pleasing qualities.

The different approaches Alice and Lucy use to get their way are typical of a stylistic variance between generations. Alice, who has so little power, is furtive. Her experience taught her that the way to get what she wants in a world where men call the shots and pay the bills is to maneuver behind the scenes. Lucy, who has considerable power and grew up when "openness" came to be considered more important than good manners, is direct. Women of Lucy's generation don't have to be as subtle or hide their agendas because they know that they can make their own way in the world. But directness can seem disrespectful to a generation that was brought up to believe that being blunt is rude. Although Alice's manipulativeness is irritating, Lucy's "top sergeant" approach is a setup for resistance. Sometimes just the style with which a daughter tries to help her parents solve their problems makes them want to tune her out.

A generation gap in the values about what constitutes an admirable life also interferes with Lucy's respect for her mother. Although Alice never worked or traveled, she brought up two successful daughters who are responsible and loving, she and Daniel have an exceptionally companionable marriage, and Alice had a long run as a soloist in her amateur choral group. Measured by the goals Alice set when she was a young woman—to be a good wife, mother, and member of the community—she has succeeded. It's not her fault that her daughter's generation has different aims.

There is no financial pressure on Lucy to insist that her parents make a major change, and she has come around to deciding that what is "best" for them is to design their own way of life. Instead of trying to calm her anxiety by placing her parents in a "safe" place, she has begun to use her resourcefulness to help them to stay at home. Because Lucy pays whoever takes care of her parents, she will attempt to set the ground rules about hours and duties and oversee the caretaker rather than expect Alice or Daniel to do it. That might work or it might not, and it won't relieve Lucy and her sister of the day-to-day responsibilities the way the assisted-living facility would, but it can alleviate some of the family tension.

If Lucy can live with her anxiety about her parents and let Alice know that she respects her desire to stay in her home—and that she will work with her to make that a practical choice—her relationship with Alice will probably become less adversarial.

Then, if either Daniel's or Alice's health deteriorates so badly that they really can't live at home—or if Daniel dies and Alice is alone—Alice might be more open to accepting Lucy's collaboration in helping her decide where and how to lead the next phase of her life. But as circumstances change, Lucy may have to keep reminding herself that what she wants for her mother and what Alice wants for herself may be different and that sometimes there isn't a single "right" solution.

When a daughter makes it clear, as Lucy did, that she feels she has a more realistic sense than her parents do of what would be best for them, it can activate a mother's belief that she is losing control over her own life. An older person who has to leave her home not only is losing a place with deep associations but also sometimes must acknowledge that the reason she is moving reflects another loss: of the abilities that allow her to live the way she always has.

The feeling of powerlessness as choices narrow—a combination of the actual effects of age and others' perception of the way age has diminished her—is among the most distressing effects of growing older.

Good communication, honesty, and a relationship that is less fraught with anxiety can help a mother and daughter make important decisions together. That was the case with Peggy and her mother, Dana.

~

PEGGY AND DANA

"We were able to talk it out."

Peggy and Dana had worked hard to understand and respect each other as adults. By the time they sat down to make plans for Dana's later years, they both felt confident that neither of them would try to impose her point of view on the other, and they could listen carefully without a lot of emotional static interfering with the reception.

Dana had asked Peggy to meet with her and her lawyer to discuss the terms of Dana's will, of which Peggy was the principal beneficiary. As such meetings often do, the subjects covered included a living will, a power of attorney, and other projections about the future. What could have been an acrimonious discussion was calm and respectful and actually improved Peggy and Dana's relationship, but it had taken them both quite a bit of adjustment to reach that point.

"Mom and I didn't always get together about things," Peggy says. "I'm a playwright and that's not a very secure way to make a living. After I got divorced and had to support myself, my career used to be a real point of contention between us.

"At first, Mom used to tell me I should get a 'real' job until she realized how hard I work—pretty much seven days a week. Then I invited her to a rehearsal of one of my off-Broadway plays. Her perspective changed when she saw that the other people I was working with respected me. It helped when I got some good reviews, too. Now, if I *don't* get great notices, Mom will get very defensive and say the critic missed the point. Once I had to beg her not to write a letter to the newspaper. 'How would that sound, Mom?' I said. 'You're going to tell him he misunderstood your daughter?' So she's stopped telling me to get a job. If she does make a suggestion, she's more likely to say, 'I wish you didn't have to work all the time and could have some fun.'

"Her real fear is that I'm going to meet an actor who is even less financially stable than I am," Peggy says, and grins. "She's put a lot of what she's leaving me in a trust; I think it's to protect me from this mythological actor, in case he comes along. My initial reaction was that the trust was a symbol that Mom doesn't trust *me*, but she just wants to be certain I'm secure."

When Peggy, Dana, and the lawyer began to talk about future contingencies, Peggy asked Dana under what circumstances she might consider moving out of her apartment into a communal arrangement. Dana would have to leave New York City, where she has lived all her life, as there are very few options for upper-middle-income assisted living in Manhattan. Dana had always said, as many older people do, "I'd rather die than go to a nursing home." Peggy asked her if she felt that way about other forms of adult community.

"I'm not saying it's a good idea to move," she told Dana, "but we haven't really talked about it and this seems like a good time."

Dana didn't feel that her daughter was pressuring her, so rather than snapping, "Never!" she began to talk about the community where her cousin lives, in New Hampshire. "It's run by the Quakers, and there's no alcohol served in the public rooms," she said. "That isn't very sociable. And even though the people are nice, they're a little unsophisticated. Her apartment is pretty, but so is mine. On the whole," she said, "I don't see what the benefit would be of moving. It wouldn't make things easier for you, either, because you'd have to travel to see me."

Dana asked the lawyer, who specializes in trusts and estates, if he could estimate the difference between the cost of living in a community where medical services would be available if she became sick or disabled and the cost of staying home with nursing care. "I don't want to spend much of my capital," she said. "I want to be sure Peggy is taken care of when she gets to be my age, if she can't work." The lawyer, who had experience in similar situations, assured both Dana and Peggy that, unless Dana became seriously demented or had a severe medical condition that required institutionalization, home care would cost about the same as living in a partial-care community. Her current income, he said, would cover both possibilities.

But, he asked, if Dana lost her mental faculties to a considerable degree, would she trust Peggy to determine at what point she could no longer be cared for at home? Dana answered without hesitation that she did.

"We were able to talk it out. My mother was reassured that we understood what she wanted and that she could afford it," Peggy says. "It makes it easier for me to respect the way she would like to live because she learned to respect my choices about my own life."

These two daughters, Peggy and Lucy, brought very different histories to the same question: Where should an aging, but not infirm, mother live?

Lucy didn't realize that the decision she was trying to make for her parents reflected more about her anxiety and discomfort with ambiguity than with her parents' actual needs. She was trying to calm her fears, and she was punishing her mother for passing along her predisposition to worry rather than rationally considering the options. When a daughter feels overly emotional about a parent's decision, she may be absolutely right. Her reaction may be a signal that her parents really are on the road to disaster. But strong feelings can also indicate that the problem is in the relationship, not the practical situation. A daughter would do well to step back and analyze why she is reacting with such heat before she takes an adversarial stand that might damage her relationship with her mother even further.

Peggy and Dana had done a lot of the work of coming to terms with each other before any decision had to be made, so Dana could think out loud without feeling too exposed. Lucy and Alice can still reach an understanding like the one Peggy and Dana have if Lucy can reassure her mother that she has learned from the "luxury hotel" experience to respect her wishes.

CHAPTER 11

❧

Balancing Duty and Self-Preservation

Abusive Mothers

A mother's point of view is almost always an important consideration; no relationship can flourish unless both people are sensitive to each other's feelings. But there is an exception: when a mother is abusive, her daughter has to put her own survival ahead of her mother's wishes.

The balance between self-interest and selflessness is never easy to maintain. When we get it wrong, if we are too selfish, we feel guilty. Sometimes we feel guilty even when we do the *right* thing because we resent what we have to give up to do it or because we can't make our mothers' lives as comfortable as we would like. Daughters of abusive mothers have a particularly hard time balancing duty and self-preservation while holding guilt at bay.

Ironically, mothers who are not good enough often evoke a particularly powerful sense of guilt in their children. A child who is not adequately loved or who has been abused almost invariably thinks it is her fault—that she is not lovable enough. (Husbands who abuse their wives often persuade them that it's their fault, too, that they have so severely provoked the men that they deserve to be hit.) So when an abusive mother becomes an *old and ill* abusive mother, her daughter is likely to bring a disproportionate measure of guilt to any decisions she makes about how to deal with her. The daughter of such a mother can try to maintain emotional equilibrium by establishing a carefully calibrated distance or, in extreme situations, cutting off contact entirely. But because she is less loving and attentive than other women are to *their* mothers, the guilt she is carrying around may begin to feel very heavy.

Practical problems can make difficult relationships worse. If a mother is sick or poor, her daughter may simply not be able to stand to abandon her to a life of misery. (The fantasy that her mother's neediness will make her softer or change her behavior pattern can be a seductive inducement to keep on trying.) And a daughter who decides to cut her mother off is admitting that there is no hope.

Being dutiful might help a daughter prove to herself that she is not like her mother, and that could be enough reason to take on a task that is rather like swimming in waters infested with stinging jellyfish—painful but not lethal. But for some daughters, the price of assuaging their guilt is too much like diving into a tank with a killer shark. Moira's mother, Addie, who had physically and emotionally abused her, falls into the killer shark category, but by the time Addie had become totally incapacitated, Moira had developed enough strength to feed the shark without becoming dinner herself.

~

MOIRA AND ADDIE

"When my mother finally died, I was relieved."

The phone rang, but Moira's teenage daughters, Jenny and Anne, didn't pick it up. They were screening the calls, so if it was their grandmother Addie—and it was—she could complain to the tape rather than to them. They stood over the answering machine, looking at it and listening while their grandmother left her message. Then they raised their eyebrows at each other and went back to their homework.

When Moira got home around nine that night after working at her second job, she played back her mother's message. Then she erased the tape, made herself a cup of tea, and thought about Addie. Even at the end of a two-job day, with her hands around a cup of tea and her curly red hair pushed behind her ears, Moira had the competent, determined posture of a woman who could handle anything. Handling her mother meant refusing to listen to Addie's abuse, especially when Moira was tired and her defenses were low.

How bad could Addie have been that her daughter and granddaughters dreaded even hearing her voice? Very bad, indeed.

"When my mother finally died, I was relieved," Moira says. "One more link to my childhood cut. Growing up, it was just chaos. Six of us living in a five-room apartment, waiting for the next outbreak of violence. My father was an alcoholic, and he beat up my mother and us kids, too, especially when he was drinking."

Addie didn't drink as much as her husband, Joe, but she was just as mean. Often she started the fights that escalated into free-for-alls, with both parents striking out at each other and the children. Sometimes when Joe was attacking her, Addie would try to deflect his attention to one of their children. Other times, even when she was the instigator, she would call the police.

In addition to the beatings, Joe sexually molested all the children except Moira, who was prone to convulsions. "I think my father was afraid that if he abused me too much it would kill me, and then he'd be held for murder," Moira says. Her convulsions were misdiagnosed as symptoms of an inoperable brain tumor and not correctly diagnosed as a treatable, less severe condition until Moira was in her twenties. "The misdiagnosis probably saved my life," she says. Moira tried to protect her brothers and sister from their father by begging her mother to intervene, but Addie's response was to become enraged, tell Moira she was imagining things, and punish her.

The physical abuse was laced with other kinds of mistreatment. "When I was as young as seven," Moira says, "my mother used to send me to the bar to tell my father to come home. Or he would drink up the food money, and my mother would send me to the grocery store to beg for some milk.

"It sounds like a poor-childhood cliché, but the strange thing—well, there were a lot of strange things—is that my father was able to hide his drinking and his violence well enough to keep a good job for a long time. He was a sergeant in the army; we had pictures of him all over the house, in his uniform, wearing his medals."

Addie's terrible performance as a mother was understandable, if not excusable: she spent nine years of her childhood in a home for abandoned children, left school in the eighth grade, and was married and a mother at seventeen. She saw Joe, with his army career, as her chance for security. When he turned out to be violent, she didn't have the resources to leave him.

Despite her behavior, Addie, who had never experienced a good mother herself, "used to tell us that she was the best mother, the only one who could take care of us and protect us from our father and everything else out there in the world," Moira says.

"All of us children were terrified that one day Dad would kill her, and then there wouldn't be anyone to protect us. She really convinced us that she was our protector."

Moira managed to get away. As soon as she graduated from high school, she found a job, moved out of her parents' house, and took college courses at night. But, she says, "I was still going home a lot because my mother told me that's what a good daughter does and because my younger brothers and sister were having problems. They believed what my mother told them, that she would take care of them, so they stayed close to her and took what she handed out, which was mostly abuse and orders." By then, both brothers had begun to be sucked into alcoholism, and Moira's younger sister clung to their mother.

"I was really on my own if I wanted to get anywhere with my life," Moira says, "although I made some mistakes at the beginning." Among them was marrying a man who also turned out to be an alcoholic. Soon after their second daughter was born, they were divorced, and Moira's husband faded out of her life. By then, Moira could support herself and her children. She had her bachelor's degree and was working at the two jobs she still holds, as an office manager in a real estate company and running a bed-and-breakfast in one of the houses the company owns.

"Okay," Moira says. "Fast-forward. My father dies. My mother gets adult-onset diabetes. Now my mother wants us over there all the time. She's very religious, and she wants us to go to Sunday Mass with her every week. I've got to cook dinner at my apartment, take the food and my daughters to her house on the subway, go to Mass, then go back and eat the dinner I cooked, clean up and wash the dishes, and bring my stuff home on the subway.

"Then she gets *really* sick and *now* she wants me to go over there three times a week. But I live an hour away, I've got these two jobs, and my kids are in school."

Moira still found it hard to say no to Addie because she was the only one of the siblings who was reliable and stable. "My sister was married by then, but even though she was at my mother's more than she was at her own place, she wasn't much help. She's scared of everything, and she was terrified of Mom," Moira says. "As for the boys, they were useless. It was up to us girls to take care of my mother, and she was in such bad shape, it was practically impossible *not* to do."

When Addie's diabetes had progressed so far that she had to have a leg amputated, Moira went to the hospital to see her every day. On the night Moira's daughters were standing over the answering machine, listening to Addie's message, Addie was calling from the hospital where she had had her other leg amputated. She had already called Moira at work five times that day, and Moira had spoken to her each time.

"My mother conditioned me to do what she wanted. She said a good daughter obeys her mother. If I didn't do what was expected of me, my mother physically and psychologically punished me," Moira says. "I was tormented by guilt because I wasn't running up to see her in the hospital all the time, but I told myself that I had to be a good mother, too, and that I had other responsibilities. I'm a daughter, but I'm also an adult.

"It isn't always easy to keep that in mind. I grew up thinking a daughter should be guided by her mother. If I didn't listen to her, I wouldn't have the guidance of a mother, and that's scary," Moira says.

Even now, Moira can't stand to write off her mother entirely. When she evaluates Addie's life, although she says, "She had no successes; she was a failure," she quickly adds, "But she was strong. She endured a lot." And while Moira insists that she is not like her mother, explaining, "She allowed herself to become a victim; I do not," she also says, "I am strong like my mother."

Addie certainly was strong in one way: she knew how to get the attention she wanted from her children. During the four years between the time her legs were amputated and her death, "Mom was the center of the universe, with round-the-clock people taking care of her," Moira says. "She had so much power it was unbelievable.

"My mother told me that her health was failing because I didn't visit her more and I was making her depressed," Moira says. "But being ill served a purpose for her. I think she believed that if she stayed sick, she would receive attention. She might have been able to avoid the amputation, but she did the exact opposite of what the doctors told her to do, and her diabetes just got worse and worse."

When Addie had the last of a series of heart attacks, all

her children met with her doctors at the hospital. Although Addie was at the brink of death, Moira's sister and brothers begged the doctors to perform bypass surgery. "I think they were afraid that, if they let her die, she would punish them somehow," Moira says. "I told them, 'Even if you could give her another year, what kind of life is she going to have? Say what you want about me, but I vote to let her go.' Then I walked out and left them there."

The doctors told Addie's children that nothing could be done to save their mother, and a few weeks later Addie died.

Before Addie's death, Moira says, she was able to calm her guilt. "I told myself I was the best daughter I could be for her. She had stopped being a mother a long time ago—which was fine, considering the kind of mother she was. She wanted *me* to be *her* mother, but I had my own children. When she passed away and the pressure was gone, I said to myself, It's finally over.

"My mother taught us to love her because she was our mother. And after you sort it all out, I did love her in some way," Moira says. "I only wish she had said to me just once, 'I love you.' "

Healing

Although Moira followed her mother's example and punished herself by feeling guilty when she didn't do what her mother demanded, she was able to step back enough to take care of herself and her own children, rather than dropping everything to become Addie's caretaker, as Addie would have liked her to do. Addie was beyond repair; Moira had repaired herself. Part of her healing was to be the kind of mother Addie could not be; part was to be responsible about her duties as a daughter, without getting pulled into her mother's emotional morass.

Moira concludes, "When your mother is as sick as mine was, or even just housebound and dependent, it's inevitable: you're going to be dragged back in, whether it means being physically there or it's just mental, whether it's healthy or unhealthy. You have to make it clear to yourself that you're going back as an adult. You have to be able not to be drawn in as a child.

"You make your own rules; your mother is no longer the only person with the rules. As adults, we're in touch with people all the time who make us angry or upset, and we learn to deal with them. So you try to see your mother as another adult. You can still be an empathetic daughter but on your terms. You're not your mother's mother, and in as many ways as you can manage, you try to look beyond what it meant to be her child."

Really terrible mothers illustrate how deep-seated the push and pull is that underlies mother-daughter relationships. An objective observer would find it hard to forgive a mother like Addie and imagine that anyone connected to her would want to run from her as fast as possible. But Addie's daughter continued to feel the pull toward her until her death. It is hardly surprising, then, that daughters of mothers who were less overtly harmful than Addie have even more difficulty in finding ways to protect themselves from continuing damage, which can include seeing themselves as "bad daughters" if they disconnect themselves from their mothers.

A physically abusive mother like Addie is, in some ways, easier to walk away from than a mother who has inflicted less dramatic damage. Addie broke some of society's strongest taboos, those against extreme physical abuse, and she was complicitous with her husband's sexual abuse of their children. When Moira feels guilty about keeping her distance, she can tell herself that her mother's behavior was criminal. But what of daughters whose mothers have mistreated them less severely? They, too, must find a way to be good daughters to difficult mothers without being overwhelmed by the feelings that stem from a bad childhood.

The feelings of a daughter whose mother abused her more subtly under the guise that she only wanted the best for her child (and who *did* provide the best of everything material) are particularly complicated. When outward appearances are dissonant with the emotional deprivation and cruelty that take place in private, daughters sometimes wonder if they are reading their situations correctly. And women brought up in comfort are often ashamed to say that they had difficult childhoods because they are aware that so many others had neither loving mothers nor the advantages of physical luxuries and a good education.

When a mother who covertly abused her child becomes elderly, her daughter can feel as though the fog of surrealism that infected her childhood has rolled in to obscure her vision again. Lucinda's story offers some clues to why it is particularly difficult for such women to detach from their mothers and how they can manage to be good daughters to this particular breed of bad mother.

LUCINDA AND ANTOINETTE

Lucinda's mother, Antoinette, was a variation of the stage mother. She used her daughter to further her own ambitions—in this case, to travel in the "best society"—disregarding Lucinda's talents, wishes, and individuality. Yet when Antoinette was in her late sixties, had breast cancer, and became an increasingly out-of-control alcoholic, Lucinda steadfastly stood by her.

Antoinette had two daughters, Lucinda and Mathilde, but she chose Lucinda, the elder by two years and the prettier and more tractable of the girls, as the one more likely to make a brilliant match. Antoinette, who had married a man from a prominent and wealthy New Orleans family, wanted her daughters to marry either an American man with a "brand name," by which she meant that his family was known beyond the society of the city where he lived, or a European with a title. "I suppose she was insecure, but honestly, I don't care what the reason was," Lucinda says. "She made my childhood into a parody. It was like something out of Jane Austen."

Antoinette chose Lucinda's friends and her clothes and summarily dismissed any children who didn't come from the "right" families as "meaningless people." She compelled both daughters to take a battery of lessons—piano, deportment, ballet, singing, French, and riding—so they had neither the time nor the energy to develop their own interests. When Mathilde resisted following the path on which Antoinette had set Lucinda, Antoinette declared that she was a truant. Mathilde was ten when Antoinette dispatched her to a boarding school run by an order of Catholic nuns. The message was clear: go along or get sent away. Lucinda continued to go along.

When Lucinda graduated from the local private school, Antoinette sent her to a Swiss finishing school. There Lucinda met and fell in love with an attractive young titled French banker, Jean-Charles. Although Lucinda wanted to

146

go to college, Antoinette insisted that she marry her Frenchman "before he got away." Lucinda says, "He was a wonderful man, and I'm sure he would have waited for me. I was much, much too young to get married."

Still, she hoped that by living in France she could escape the most intense of her mother's attentions. "But that was only the beginning of a new phase because what she really wanted was not just for me to live in that world but for me to bring *her* into it." Unfortunately for Lucinda, her father died shortly after her marriage, leaving Antoinette with a substantial bank account and nothing to tether her to her life in the United States. So each summer and for extended holidays at Christmas and Easter, Antoinette packed her trunks and came to stay with Lucinda and Jean-Charles. "My husband was French; it's in that culture for a man to treat his mother-in-law with respect, so he put up with Mummy," Lucinda says. "But I couldn't stand having her in my house for weeks and months at a time. She used to tell me, 'This is all wasted on you. *I* am the one who should be married to Jean-Charles.'"

Lucinda and Jean-Charles had a baby girl, but within a year Lucinda finally rebelled against her mother—by abandoning the marriage for which Antoinette had groomed her. (Of course, that was only one factor; Lucinda also says, "I was too immature to be married.") Lucinda and Jean-Charles had a civil divorce and a church-approved annulment, and Lucinda and her little girl moved back to New Orleans. So did Antoinette.

Whatever thoughts Lucinda had at that point about distancing herself from her mother became impractical when Antoinette was diagnosed with breast cancer. She had to have a mastectomy, followed by radiation and chemotherapy, and she needed help. Mathilde was living in San Francisco estranged from Antoinette, so the full responsibility for her mother's care fell on Lucinda. This made it hard for her to hold the full-time job she'd found working for a decorator and to take care of her daughter—although she did both—yet Antoinette never offered to help her financially. "I think Mummy expected that if I couldn't get along on my own, I would go back to Jean-Charles, but I had closed that door firmly. Even if I had wanted to open it, I had hurt Jean-Charles too badly."

The summer Lucinda's daughter was three, the decorator she worked for asked Lucinda to spend the summer in France to oversee a project. She took her little girl with her, and she and Jean-Charles spent time together, patching up their friendship, if not their marriage. At the end of the summer, Jean-Charles offered to pay Lucinda's tuition and increase her support until she could get a college degree and a better job.

When Lucinda returned to the United States, she went to her mother's to tell her about her plans. "Mummy was in the bathtub, and she told me to come in and we could talk while she bathed. I was standing there, looking at the mastectomy scars on her chest and feeling bad for her, when Mummy said, 'Did you meet anyone in France this summer?'

"By 'anyone,' of course, she meant a man. So I said no, that I'd been working quite hard and spending the rest of the time with my daughter and sometimes with Jean-Charles. Mummy said, 'That's just what I thought. I've decided you should give the child to Jean-Charles to raise in France. You would be much more marketable without a baby hanging onto your skirts.' "

Lucinda's reaction was instantaneous. "I rushed at her and began to throttle her. I was screaming, 'Don't you ever, don't you ever!' I couldn't even finish the sentence.

I think I could have killed her. She had terrible bruises on her neck."

Yet Lucinda continued to see her mother, to answer Antoinette's calls for help late at night, when she was drunk, to go to support groups for the adult children of alcoholics, and to try—unsuccessfully—to persuade her mother to check into a professional rehabilitation program.

Before Lucinda received her college degree, Antoinette had a recurrence of cancer and learned that, even with treatment, there was very little hope that she would survive longer than a few months. Lucinda took off a semester to care for her mother; she visited her every day at home and then in the hospital. Within six months of the diagnosis, Antoinette was dead.

"I was lucky," Lucinda says. "Mummy was only in her early seventies. I could still be running over there in the middle of the night, trying to calm her down when she got into a drunken tantrum. It was a great relief to me that she went so fast, a relief, really, that she was gone.

"For about fourteen months, I was filled with rage that Mummy had been the person she was and that she had tried to mold me into this distorted shape. And then I decided that if I ever wanted to make something of myself— I mean *inside* myself—that I had to put my mother behind me. It's been nearly eleven years since she died. I think about her very rarely now."

Why was Lucinda such a good daughter? Some of the reasons she was so attentive can be traced to the way her mother brought her up. Antoinette had always given the impression that she was an exceptionally attached and attentive mother. So Lucinda, who had been taught to value appearances, was afraid she would be seen as ungrateful—

a "bad daughter"—if she wasn't more than dutiful. Antoinette trained her to be good at the things that showed—and she was. "If I had admitted that looking a certain way and knowing certain people weren't important, what would be left that I *was* good at? And since I'd made a mess of my marriage, I guess I was overcompensating because Mummy felt that I had failed her and that, in a sense, when I got divorced, she had failed, too," Lucinda says.

Lucinda hid her anger and resentment toward her mother until after Antoinette died. "Everything true was always hidden," she says. "Mummy's alcoholism, her snobbery, and, worst of all, her inability to love, which was reflected in her suggestion that I give up my child so as not to compromise my 'market value.' "

Now that Lucinda has put most of the anger behind her, she says, "I'm trying to use what Mummy taught me differently. To 'do the right thing' meant one thing to her and another to me. But whatever your reasons are, it requires discipline. And Mummy taught me to hold up my head and act like everything is fine. Sometimes that comes in handy."

Moira and Lucinda might not seem to have much in common, but they both were influenced by a daughter's innate desire to love her mother and to find something admirable in her. For Moira, it was that her mother was strong, "she prevailed." For Lucinda, it was that Antoinette's false front could be transformed into a protective surface that allowed her daughter to save her mother's pride and to act more loving than she feels.

What of women whose mothers abandoned them? Sometimes they, too, find themselves poised to step back in when their mothers age, become ill, or need financial assistance. Some hope to repair what was broken long ago. Others are showing themselves that, unlike their mothers, they are not what the English call "bolters," running away from responsibility. Some daughters are motivated by charity and forgiveness. Many hope to find out, at last, why their mothers left them.

The last attempt to reestablish a connection with a mother who disconnected herself from her children is often disappointing. That doesn't mean that a daughter shouldn't try, but if the closeness she hopes to establish doesn't materialize, she can take some consolation from knowing that the mother-daughter relationship is one boat that can't catch the wind without two sets of willing hands to raise the sails.

WENDY AND MURIEL

Wendy is a writer. A short, wrenching memoir about her experiences as a child appeared some years ago in a literary review. In that story, she makes a parallel between a damaged doll "loved" by a mentally ill cousin and her treatment by a mother who insisted that she loved Wendy and abandoned her only to "save her" from being torn apart by a custody fight.[1]

Wendy's mother, Muriel, was a college student when she fell in love with a visiting professor from a Cuban-Spanish family. Within a couple of years of their marriage, they had Wendy, but soon after, Muriel fell out of love with her husband, divorced, and became involved with another man, whom she married. Muriel turned Wendy over to her former husband; he, in turn, deposited her in Cuba with his mother and then went off to live in Spain. Wendy was twice abandoned.

Muriel and her new husband, Don, lived in New York with their two "real" children, as Wendy calls them, her half brothers, Donnie and Lars. Wendy's grandmother also had an apartment there, and Wendy saw her mother occasionally—but always at her paternal grandmother's.

"No one will ever be as glamorous as my mother in memory. She makes her entrance into my grandmother's New York apartment, wearing a dove-gray cape lined with a wine-red paisley silk that matches her dress. . . . Her lips are painted scarlet and she calls me 'Darling.' I can't take my eyes off her. I'm terrified that she'll go away," Wendy wrote. "I lived for the few times a year when my mother and I were together." Because she had never met her half brothers, "In the world that I created with my mother, no one else existed except the two of us."

When Wendy was twelve, her grandmother suffered a heart attack and, just before Christmas, Wendy was sent to visit Muriel, who had moved to Connecticut. This, Wendy thought, was the moment when she would finally become part of her mother's family. Then, as the Christmas cards began to arrive and Muriel set them on the mantel and on tables in the library, Wendy noticed that the messages written on the cards invariably said, "To Muriel and Don, with much love to the boys."

"No one mentioned me," she said, "and when my mother's friends came over, they would say things like, 'But we've never heard of you! How could Muriel have kept you a secret? Why, you're adorable!' " The part of this message, of course, that Wendy heard was not "You're adorable" but "We've never heard of you."

Her half brothers hadn't heard of her, either, until they

were about eight and ten. "For a long time, my mother had neglected to tell her sons that she had a daughter. Without my father and me, she was innocent again," Wendy wrote. Muriel used to recount the story of the "telling," turning it, as Wendy wrote, "into an anecdote about her *real* family." When told about his half sister, Donnie asked, "Why couldn't you have borned a whole one?"

"Sometimes," Wendy wrote, "she told the story in front of me and I learned to laugh with her, so that I would never be dreary and she might love me."

During her childhood, Wendy heard many versions of why her mother had abandoned her. Most of them were unsympathetic to Muriel, but Wendy chose to believe her mother's version, which turned Muriel into a self-sacrificing heroine. "If she had tried to take me with her, my father would have fought her in court. I would have suffered. She could not have lived with that. From the Bible itself came the moral authority for her choice. King Solomon would have approved of what she did, she always told me: No true mother would have allowed her child to be cut in two," Wendy wrote.

At the end of the memoir, written while her mother was alive and well, Wendy wrote that she finally had acknowledged the truth. "The crucial event of my childhood had nothing to do with King Solomon. Very simply, my mother hadn't wanted me."

Some forty years after that dismal Christmas, one of Wendy's half brothers called and told her that he thought their mother might be developing Alzheimer's disease. Wendy still saw her mother a couple of times a year, and on this occasion she offered to make an appointment for Muriel with a neurologist and to accompany her there. Muriel "flunked" the test, and Wendy and her half brothers moved her into a special nursing home when the disease progressed to a stage at which she couldn't live alone. In the course of those few years, Wendy, Donnie, and Lars began to talk about their mother, and they told her, "We used to envy you because she'd left you, and you didn't have to live with her."

"There was only one conversation we needed to have, and we never did," Wendy says. "My mother wanted me to validate her decision. I wanted her to admit that what she had done had caused me pain."

But Muriel can't have any kind of conversation with anyone now. Instead, Wendy continued her internal dialogue with herself until she finally came to a sort of resting place. "I understand that the major incident of my life was only a minor incident in *her* life. I was more like a miscarriage than a real child." A generation later, Wendy says, Muriel would have had an abortion, and Wendy would never have been born.

Wendy hasn't seen Muriel for a year; she leaves her care to Donnie and Lars and, instead, has asked her father, who is now ninety-three, to live with her and her husband. "I can help only one elderly person go from life to death. I chose my father because he loved me," Wendy says. Perhaps because in our culture we expect more of our mothers than of our fathers, we are less disappointed and angry with the fathers who are only occasional, if loving, visitors in our lives.

When Muriel's illness stripped her of the ability to interact or the power to wound her again, Wendy, like many women who have had difficult relationships with their mothers, found that she could be more philosophical.

"The battle is over," she says. "I have to see my mother in human terms, forgive her, and be sorry for the human condition, which is to grow old and die. We never resolved the original quarrel, but I think we have finished and now we have a truce that extends through eternity."

Although the truce has been signed—at least Wendy has signed her copy—when she talks about her mother, as she picks up a glass to take a sip of water, her hand is shaking. She looks down at the tremor and smiles. "Stress," she says. "It only comes out when I'm under stress."

These are extremes: battering and sexual molestation, stage mothering, and abandonment. They are, unfortunately, not rare, although they are more likely to turn up in more moderate forms. Many mothers, especially in the 1940s and 1950s, hit their children. Many still do. Mothers commonly tried to prepare their daughters to strike the jackpot in the marriage stakes, without regard to daughters' wishes. Some still do that, too. Mothers still give their children to grandparents to raise, and the modern variation on abandonment may be a mother who is so consumed with her work that she is barely involved in raising her children, except as a distant manager. But of all the forms of "bad mothering," the most common is verbal abuse, which usually takes the form of relentless criticism. Unfortunately, all children are likely to believe that their mothers know best. If what a mother "knows" and expresses is that the child is inadequate, and the criticism continues long past childhood, a daughter has some choices. She can believe her mother and give up on herself, she can continue to try to prove herself to her mother, or she can tell her mother that she is no longer entitled to criticize her, a stance that might help her heal herself. With really bad mothers, that won't do much good, of course. At that point, a daughter has to weigh the consequences of cutting off her relationship with her mother (and probably feeling guilty) against the pain of each encounter.

It's often said that a daughter with a terrible mother can't win: although every contact with her mother undermines her further, if she stays away, she will feel guilty when her mother dies. What happens when, to preserve her equilibrium—or even her sanity—a daughter "divorces" a mother who saps her emotional energy and confidence?

That's what Jane did, after her mentally unstable mother, Leila, called her a whore at a family dinner in front of Jane's young children. The incident was typical of Leila's behavior—irrational attacks that had begun when Jane was a toddler and continued throughout her life. Jane finally pulled the plug on their relationship when she accepted that there was nothing healthy she could get from staying in contact with her mother, conceded that Leila was beyond Jane's ability to help her, and acknowledged that their grandmother deeply upset her children. So Jane, in effect, amputated a limb that she couldn't save and stopped seeing her mother or answering her calls. Once she had made up her mind that there was nothing she could do to improve their relationship, Jane says she felt relieved.

Leila has been dead for a couple of years now, and Jane says, "I am glad to report that I really don't feel guilty. My mother was sadistic and cruel. Even though I know she was ill, it was hard to be sympathetic because she refused to get professional help. She used to say, 'That's the way I am. Take it or leave it.' Well, I left it, and I'd like to reassure other women who have mothers like mine that you can cut your losses and survive."

Most women don't go as far as Jane did; they manage by minimizing contact with their mothers and trying to mute their reactions when they are together. That's the way Hattie, whose mother, Madeleine, is a relentless critic, finally protected herself from overexposure to Madeleine's tongue-lashings.

~

HATTIE AND MADELEINE

"I'll never satisfy her."

Madeleine seemed to have been born with a bitter streak. For as long as Hattie can remember, she has found fault with everything—especially with her daughter. And ever since Hattie was a little girl, her reaction was always the one a critical mother is often looking for: her daughter tried harder and harder to please her.

And then one day, Hattie hit bottom. She had taken an afternoon off from her job as a librarian to shop for the ingredients Madeleine insisted she needed for a Passover dinner. Although Hattie could have gotten everything on the Upper West Side of New York, where she and her mother both lived, her mother insisted that the *best* ingredients could be found only on the Lower East Side, in a variety of stores, none of which delivered. So Hattie went from one shop to the next, assembling everything on the list, packed the groceries into a car she had borrowed, and drove uptown to her mother's apartment.

When Hattie arrived, tired but pleased with her afternoon's endeavors, Madeleine started scolding her as soon as she walked in the door. "You've gotten here so late, I'll never be able to cook it all by tomorrow night," she said, and continued to berate Hattie as she laid out the groceries on the kitchen table.

After that, Hattie made the same kind of decision Moira had, that to satisfy her own sense of duty, she would do what she thought was reasonable, but she would not expect acknowledgment from her mother.

"I'll never satisfy her," Hattie said, "so I decided to make my own definition of a good daughter. As long as I meet my standards, that will have to be enough."

Now Hattie sees her mother considerably less but calms her conscience by calling her more often. Sometimes she sends her a little gift. "My mother finds fault with everything I do," Hattie says, "but at least now I hear on the *phone* that the panty hose I sent ran the first time she wore them. I don't have to sit in her kitchen and look at the ripped hose she saved to show me what an incompetent shopper I am."

Like Moira, Hattie was determined to prove that she was different from her mother by doing the right thing, but both of them were able to limit the amount of abuse they allowed themselves to be exposed to. This is a difficult and exhausting prescription, and not every daughter can manage to stay the course. When a woman like Jane has to shut her mother out of her life, only a mother like Leila would blame her.

Bad mothers not only ruin their children's childhoods but also deprive them of the chance to become good daughters when their mothers age. This need appears to be deeper than we might have thought. When we realize what daughters like Moira, Wendy, Hattie, and Jane have missed, it highlights the importance of every stage in the mother-daughter relationship. Women with really bad mothers never have the chance to rectify wrongs and develop better relationships with their mothers that can help close the circle, the way other women do. What they can do is develop the extra strength it takes to break the cycle of abusive or unloving mothering—either by taking care of their mothers in their old age or by becoming responsible and loving mothers themselves. And sometimes the only way to move on in a constructive way is to sever the ties entirely.

CHAPTER 12

❧

Living Together, Staying Independent

Tough Choices

Most mothers and daughters don't want to live together. Only one-fifth of older people who need care live with their caregiver. Of those who live in the same household, 69 percent do so because the older person needs too much assistance with activities of daily living to live on her own.[1] Even then, deciding to ask an elderly mother to move in can be a tough choice.

In addition to the practical responsibilities, a daughter's biggest challenge when she and her mother share a home can be to avoid falling back into old mother-child patterns of interaction. A daughter can set a more adult model by treating her mother with respect and consideration and insisting on the same treatment for herself. Some mothers will follow a daughter's example or take the initiative, but others are undermined by their dependency or have never learned to set their own boundaries.

Because parents usually don't move in with an adult

child unless they need daily assistance, this arrangement is often the last attempt to stave off the step most people dread: going to a nursing home. Unlike assisted-living and other communities, nursing homes serve people who are physically too frail or ill to care for themselves and who usually require the kind of professional medical attention that only the rich can afford at home. Some nursing homes are superbly run, attractively appointed, and staffed by kind, attentive, and professional nurses, doctors, and aides. A few fulfill the nightmare vision of helpless, bedridden older people who are neglected and treated cruelly. Most do as well as they can for people who may be in pain, depressed, and severely limited in their ability to get much out of life. The common explanation, "I had to *put* my mother in a nursing home," succinctly describes two of the essential components of the situation: "had to," as in "had no choice," and "put," with its overtones of a package stored in a cupboard.

Grace and her mother, Mary Rose, experienced both stages: first, Mary Rose moved in with Grace. Then Mary Rose's health deteriorated so severely that she needed full-time care which Grace, who worked, couldn't provide, and Grace had to move her into a nursing home. The situation could have been different for both of them if their relationship had been more equal. Grace sacrificed a great deal to help her mother, but the quality of both their lives might have been better if Grace had taken a tougher stance.

~

GRACE AND MARY ROSE

"I will curse you from my grave for this."

When you visit Grace at her apartment in Florida, she might show you where she keeps the ashes. Mary Rose's ashes are in a little vaselike container on top of the television because, Grace says, watching TV was her mother's last pleasure. Of course, this means that when Grace turns on the television she and the ashes come face to face, and that confrontation reminds Grace of certain things, such as what her mother said to her when Grace took her to the nursing home. A second urn contains Grace's daughter's ashes, and it is carefully placed at the center of Grace's bureau in the bedroom. Grace's eldest child was killed in a car crash more than a decade ago. "She was nineteen," Grace says. "The same age I was when I had her." It is hard not to think of Grace, looking at the urn on the dresser and then at herself in the mirror.

Grace, who is in her early fifties, lives alone now; her other two children, a son and daughter, are both grown and out of the house. In the winters, Grace is in Florida; in the summers, she drives north to New England in her red convertible. This life following the sun is not one of luxury; Grace owns and operates two hairdressing salons, both in seasonal resorts, and she works ten- and twelve-hour days, six days a week. In the winter, her clients are mostly elderly; summers, she often takes care of three or even four generations in the same family.

Grace has heard plenty of stories from older mothers and their daughters about how they love or fail each other.

162

When asked, she can give sound, practical advice. Yet when Grace's mother became dependent on her, much of what she had observed among her clients didn't apply because her financial resources limited her options. The economic constraints, combined with Grace's relationship with her mother, set her up for two difficult situations: living together and a life that ends in a nursing home.

Grace hasn't had an easy time, but she has a cheerful manner—although sometimes her high spirits can seem slightly nervous because she so clearly wants to please. She doesn't have much camouflage, which means that she also isn't very well protected. The three men she married (and then divorced) must have been attracted to her good nature—she laughs easily, and her big blue eyes have a mischievous quality. Her hair is dark brown, short, wavy, well coiffed, and natural; her nails are perfectly manicured and, on days when she isn't doing someone else's nails, lacquered red. Her eyeglass frames are red, too. That's her color, the color of fun, she'll tell you.

Mary Rose was once fun-loving, too, Grace says. "When my parents were first dating, my mother was a wing-walker on my father's small plane. She was a tiny little thing, five feet tall, shiny black hair." But once Grace, the first of her five children, was born, Mary Rose never got in—or on—a plane again. What's more, she never learned to drive a car.

Most of Mary Rose's life during the first twenty years of her marriage to Grace's father, Bill, consisted of hard work. Four children, all boys, followed Grace. "Mom raised us on an allowance from my father of fifty dollars a week," Grace reports. "Somehow, she took good care of us, at least as far as cooking and cleaning. She still had some of her party spirit; there were always a lot of people in the house. Mom was good-hearted and fun-loving; I guess I inherited it from her."

As often happens in large families, Grace, as the eldest child, quickly learned both to take care of herself and to help with the younger children. Mary Rose focused her interest on the boys, and the more independent Grace became, the less attention her mother paid her.

"I have a shelf of awards for debate and drama, but neither of my parents came to the school plays or ceremonies," Grace says. If her parents had encouraged her or even noticed her talent, she thinks she would have tried to become an actress, but they didn't. "They couldn't even get to my graduation. My father owned and ran two gas stations, so he worked all the time, and my mother had the four boys at home. Since she never learned to drive, she didn't have any way to get to my school."

Mary Rose never talked to Grace about men, and Grace says, "I sort of had to figure it out by myself. My mother was really bound to my father, but I think he had a couple of girlfriends. I remember as a young child, dropping off a note to some lady for him at a restaurant." Grace speculates that her unsuccessful marriages may have been a reaction to the way her father treated her mother. "I hate relationships," she says, and then laughs and admits, "although I guess I've had a lot of them."

By the time Grace was nineteen, she was pregnant. She was a practicing Catholic who never considered doing anything other than having the baby and marrying the father of her child. That didn't mollify Mary Rose. "She was really angry with me," Grace says. "I think she was afraid that I would have the same kind of life she had."

Grace married but soon divorced her first husband and

supported her daughter by working as a manicurist. By then, her younger brothers were grown and had left home, and Mary Rose, whose anger with Grace passed when Grace's child was born, had more time to spend with her. She and Grace went to New York on a couple of trips and down to "a little shack" in the Florida Keys that Mary Rose's father had bought for vacations. "We had fun together," Grace says, "although we still didn't talk about much."

Grace married again and had two more children, but that marriage didn't work out, either. Then she was married for the third time: that husband was a hairdresser, and they opened their own salon together. For the first time, Grace's financial condition was not precarious, her children were doing well in school, and her relationship with her mother was reasonably good.

And then, around the time Mary Rose turned fifty, "she seemed to give up," Grace says. "It may have been menopause, but whatever it was, suddenly her mood changed and she became withdrawn and depressed. She gained weight and lost teeth. And she was afraid of doctors and dentists, so she didn't get much health care."

Grace's father had retired; his health wasn't great, either, but he was well enough that Grace didn't feel that she had to take charge. Her brothers all lived nearby, and among them, her parents had enough attention.

Then Grace's eldest daughter died. Grace was working, raising the two younger children, trying to make her third marriage better than the ones that had come before—and grieving. She didn't have much time to spend with her parents or worry about them until her father had a heart attack and died in his sleep.

Mary Rose had a little surge of energy after her husband's death. Although she was sad, she was also briefly elated because she discovered that he had saved sixty thousand dollars, which he had hidden in the house. "Let's go shopping!" she said to Grace. "For a while she had a bit of her old twinkle back," Grace says, "but it didn't last. She couldn't cope. She let her teeth go and she was just a mess. My mother never took care of herself, never looked great. Maybe that's why I'm in the beauty business, to make everybody look fabulous and have fun."

It wasn't just Mary Rose's moods and her appearance that were poor. Her health had begun to disintegrate, too. "She had a bad back; nobody knew why. Then she had an aortic aneurysm, and then she broke a hip," Grace says. "The doctors told me that, with physical therapy, Mom would be able to walk pretty well, but she refused. She said, 'I'm too old to learn to walk all over again. You can wheel me around.' Once Mom even said she wished they made baby carriages for bigger people."

Grace's brothers were used to letting their big sister take care of things, as she always had. They might have been more helpful if she had told them that she needed them, but Grace just kept reporting on their mother's condition and what she was doing for her, and they continued to stop by and see Mary Rose when it was convenient for them and to chip in some money when they thought of it.

Grace didn't ask for help from her brothers, and she didn't stand up to her mother, either. Instead of telling Mary Rose that she was on her own if she didn't try the physical therapy, Grace bought her mother a wheelchair. Then she asked Mary Rose to move in with her. There was room in her apartment again: Grace and her third husband had gotten divorced, and her son was away at college.

Living together wasn't so bad at the beginning. Mary Rose and Grace's younger daughter, Polly, were close. "Mom adored Polly, who thought she was a hoot, and they had a great time together, so that was good for both of them," Grace says. Mary Rose's presence sometimes was also good for Grace, who was building a new business, establishing her own salons after the split with her husband; her days were long, and she was tired after work. Mary Rose couldn't do much around the house because she was in a wheelchair and of a mind to be waited on, but she had always liked to cook. At first, she often made dinner. "Classic American home cooking," Grace says, "turkey, mashed potatoes. But before long, she lost interest, and the turkey was replaced by frozen turkey breast and the potatoes came out of a box."

Cooking wasn't the only thing that failed to capture Mary Rose's interest. She was passive about everything. "I kept trying to cheer her up, get a smile," Grace says. "We went out to lunch together, did a little shopping, or I would take her for a ride to the beach." Each of these outings was physically arduous. First Grace would wheel her mother to the station wagon, help her into the front seat, wheel the chair to the back of the vehicle, collapse the chair, and hoist it in. When they got to their destination, she would reverse the process. She did the whole thing all over again when they were ready to leave, and one more time when they got home—in and out, four times.

Mary Rose read a lot, but "mostly junk," and she watched television all day. "That's when I really stopped respecting her," Grace admits. "She just wasn't living any kind of life." She pauses, as though she feels uncomfortable about criticizing her mother, then adds, "She was a very basic, pleasant person. Not annoying. Whatever we

167

wanted to do, wherever we wanted to go, she would say, 'Fine.' She was easy to get along with. We never fought or argued; Mom didn't get angry. I don't, either."

But Mary Rose complained incessantly, often about her health. "Although Mom was preoccupied with her health," Grace says, "she had a love-hate relationship with doctors. She was scared to go to them, and she would put off going and break appointments, but she was always talking about her medications and what was wrong with her. I can't believe the pills her doctors gave her. They never even checked to see what else she was taking. When she died, she had a bag full of pills hidden under her mattress. I never want to be like that; I hate to take even an Advil."

Mary Rose's ambivalence about doctors led to a serious condition that could have been averted if she had addressed it earlier. "She had a leaky bowel condition, but she refused to see anyone about it," Grace says. "Finally, one night the pain was so severe, I took her to the emergency room. The doctors said it was too far along to treat. They had to give her a colostomy."

When Mary Rose came back to Grace's apartment, she had a colostomy bag, which she either couldn't or wouldn't change herself. Grace tried to change the bag, but it made her feel sick. One of her sisters-in-law said it didn't bother her and offered to come over and change the bag, but that didn't work because she didn't live close enough and the bag had to be changed too often.

"Finally, it was impossible to keep her at home," Grace says. "Even with my brothers' financial help, we couldn't afford a home-care aide for the amount of time my mother needed. So my brothers and I agreed to put her in the nursing home, and we shared the cost."

But they didn't share the unpleasant task of moving

their mother into the nursing home. Mary Rose felt that her daughter was throwing her out to die, and she was furious. As Grace was wheeling her into the home, Mary Rose turned around and spat over her shoulder, "I will curse you from my grave for this. I will come back to haunt you."

Grace tried to assuage her guilt by moving to an apartment close to the nursing home so she could visit every day and take her mother out when Mary Rose felt well enough to go. A bonus was that the apartment was across the street from a better school for Polly, who dropped in regularly to see her grandmother.

"Mom was right about the nursing home," Grace says. "It wasn't a bad place, but every day when I went to see her, I would hear crying coming from some room or other. It was that sort of thin wail a baby makes when it knows no one is going to come and take care of it, but it's too miserable not to cry anyway."

"One good thing was, when you're in bed and you can't go anywhere, it's hard to avoid talking," Grace says. "I finally told my mother that I was ashamed that I had been married so many times. It always bothered me and I figured she didn't respect me for it, but she said, 'That's all right. I would have divorced your father long ago, but I couldn't, because I didn't know how to drive.' Then she told me she envied my life and my independence. It helped a lot."

Mary Rose lived in the nursing home for two years. Then, one night she died in her sleep the way her husband had, of an aneurysm.

The day after Mary Rose's funeral, Grace drove down to a car dealer in the station wagon she had bought to transport her mother's wheelchair and traded in the wagon for that red convertible.

But she is still upset that her mother had to spend her last years in the nursing home. "I can't forgive myself for not coming up with a way to keep her home until the end," Grace says. "My grandmother was really sick when she was old, and she lived with my parents until she died. I have always thought there must have been something I could have done to keep my mother out of that place."

Trying Too Hard to Please

A daughter like Grace, who hasn't gotten much approval or attention from her mother, can have a hard time finding the confidence to build her own identity because she is still trying so hard to get her mother's attention. Grace needed to be a perfect daughter because Mary Rose wasn't a good enough mother. But Grace might have been able to make different choices that would have disrupted her life less if she had understood the extent to which her shame about her failures and her guilt that she couldn't fix everything for her mother were set into motion by Mary Rose's negligence and neediness.

Grace hoped her model behavior as a responsible, companionable, and loving daughter would finally inspire Mary Rose to acknowledge her. Instead of giving herself credit for the ways she had prevailed, Grace was still waiting for her mother to absolve her for her mistakes and recognize her successes. As she worked harder and harder to please Mary Rose and received so little recognition, her mother confirmed Grace's opinion of herself as a woman who couldn't do even the "right" thing right.

Grace couldn't change Mary Rose's personality, but she could have changed her own reaction to it. Instead of trying to earn the approval her mother evidently was incapable of offering, she might have focused her attention on creating a balance between what her mother needed and what she could reasonably give her.

She might also have insisted that her brothers share more of the responsibility. For example, Grace could have asked her brothers to take Mary Rose out on a regular schedule. Grace and her brothers could also have pooled their resources to consult a geriatric counselor, who might have reassured Grace and put her in touch with services that would help Mary Rose so that she would not be as entirely dependent on her daughter. For a family that hasn't been able to talk out problems, a professional counselor can provide a safe way to bring issues into the open and provide models for frank discussions in which everyone can express a point of view without threatening the family equilibrium.

Some of the practical problems could have been averted if Grace had developed enough self-respect to say no. For example, Grace could have told her mother that she would drive her to rehabilitation but she wouldn't chauffeur her anywhere else unless she agreed to try to learn to walk again. But Grace's dismay that she could never please her mother enough to get a positive reaction prevented her from setting boundaries earlier. If she had insisted that her mother meet her halfway, at least in the practical aspects of her life, rather than letting Mary Rose get away with doing so little, Grace could have improved not only her own life but also probably her mother's.

If Mary Rose had been unable to walk even after therapy, Grace and her brothers could have looked at possibilities other than having Mary Rose live with Grace and Polly, before Grace's physical condition had deteriorated to the point where she had to go into a nursing home. At that stage she might have been able to stay in a less extreme (and less depressing) residential situation for those who are partly disabled but still active. Grace and Polly wouldn't have been Mary Rose's principal sources of entertainment, and in such a community Mary Rose's "party spirit" might have revived.

Because medical care would have been right there, rather than an appointment and a car ride away, Mary Rose might have seen a doctor about her leaky bowel condition before it became so severe. As women of our generation know because we were toilet trained when women didn't talk about "bodily functions," many of our mothers were raised to consider it unladylike and embarrassing to discuss certain subjects, among them, defecation and menstruation. (One woman, entering menopause, asked her elderly mother how she and her friends had dealt with their symptoms. Her mother, who had had a hysterectomy and taken hormone replacements, looked puzzled. "None of my friends had any symptoms," she said. "The only one I can think of is Leslie. We knew she was getting hot flashes because her face turned beet red.") Since menopause and its symptoms are openly discussed—sometimes obsessively—by baby boomers and we know that hardly anyone escapes some side effects of the body's change, we can surmise that our mothers decided to suffer in silence. And that's often the way they continue to suffer as they age, especially when symptoms of ill health are concentrated between the waist and the thighs.

Mary Rose was particularly unprepared to deal with the bad hand old age dealt her. Her hard life had worn her out, and she had never been treated for her depression and only sporadically for her other illnesses. By the time she began to show the signs of aging and infirmity, even though she wasn't chronologically very old, she was too depleted to cope and decided it was her turn to have someone wait on her. It was reasonable for Grace to want to give Mary Rose what she needed. But Grace didn't know where or how to stop, so she went too far because of what *she* needed.

Grace couldn't confront the real issues—depression, exhaustion, and dependence—underlying Mary Rose's deterioration because her agenda was still the agenda of a child (Look at me! Praise me!).

Even women with more sensitive, responsive mothers sometimes feel the same way. Although parents who brought up their children after World War II were usually not nearly as strict and formal as *their* parents had been, certain beliefs from the prior generation continued, among them that praising a child too much would give her "a swelled head" and spoil her. Even parents who acknowledged and encouraged their children's accomplishments usually held back from making too much of a fuss about them. (That's not surprising: our mothers were brought up in an era when Dr. John B. Watson, the principal child development expert, made the chilling recommendation, "Never kiss your child. . . . Never hold it in your lap. Never rock its carriage.")[2]

Other women raised in the postwar era by mothers more attentive than Mary Rose also feel uncertain about their mothers' love and respect. Like Grace, they may continue to seek approval from mothers who do admire them but are programmed not to express their admiration.

Daughters whose mothers really have loved or respected them too little often try too hard to please their mothers and "love" them too much. It is as though humans require a certain amount of love (which may well be the case); if the necessary amount could be measured, and it was, say, two cups, and a mother is capable of producing only half a cup, the daughter may try to make up the difference by supplying a cup and a half and offering the extra to her mother—or her own children.

That is not always a bad solution, especially if a daughter is showing herself that she doesn't have to be like her mother. But if a daughter hopes that her love and attention will change a person who has been stingy in the love department all her life, the odds are that the daughter will be disappointed. Some mothers are undemonstrative. Others are cracked vessels; no matter how much love their daughters pour into them, it will seep out, and the vessel will have to be refilled again and again. That doesn't mean a daughter should stop pouring, but she will do better if she considers the act of loving its own reward and doesn't go into overproduction in the hope of a return that is unlikely to come.

AMY AND NINA

"It took a while for us to sort some things out."

Mothers and daughters who start out with a respectful friendship can reach a gratifying new level of affection and understanding when they share a household as adults. When Amy and her husband, David, invited Amy's mother, Nina, to live with them after Nina broke her arm in a fall on the ice, they were able to coexist without much friction because they had a history of treating each other as separate adults who are entitled to privacy and respect. Amy and Nina would both tell you that living together provided an opportunity to advance their relationship.

Amy was concerned that if Nina came to live with them, Nina would feel like a "fifth wheel," and that she and David wouldn't have enough time alone. Nina was reluctant to move in with her daughter and son-in-law for the same reasons. She proposed a six-month trial period to see if the arrangement would work. During that period, she would rent her house for income but would not sell it, in case she wanted to move back. The fact that there was an escape clause—and that Nina had suggested it—reduced the pressure on everyone from the start.

Nina also proposed that, most nights, she would eat her dinner in the kitchen before David and Amy came home from work, so she wouldn't have an obtrusive profile in the household. As it developed, she usually joined her daughter and son-in-law for a glass of wine before they ate, to hear their news and tell them hers. Then she went upstairs to her room to read or watch television, while David and Amy had dinner together.

"It took a while for us to sort some things out," Amy says. "For example, David and I both work, and we always did errands on Saturday morning. Since my mother couldn't drive anymore, she often had a little list of things for us to do for her. When we didn't find what she wanted, we decided we weren't going to spend half the morning looking for something if she didn't need it right away. The first time that happened, I felt the way I used to when the children were little and I went on a business trip and didn't bring them presents—as though Santa skipped our house.

"With the kids, I learned to tell them the truth, that I didn't have time and that the purpose of a business trip was not to go shopping. I told my mother pretty much the same thing: we have only that one day to do our errands and we will do our best. I think she was relieved that I recognized that she was considerate enough not to want us to waste the day looking for a book that was out of stock when she still had three books she hadn't read yet."

After the six months were over, Nina, Amy, and David sat down together and talked about what had worked and what was still not so great about their arrangement.

"I asked Mom to talk first," Amy says, "so she wouldn't think we were 'grading' her. She had a few suggestions about ways she could feel more at home; we had some ideas, too. Overall, we decided that we all liked living together enough to continue. Mom suggested we give it another six months; I think she may have been hoping she would be strong enough to move back into her house, which she missed. That never happened, though. Mom fell again, and this time she broke her hip. She moved into a community for older people on a short-term basis while she was in rehab. Sort of the same six-month idea. She was happy there, and she decided to stay."

A relationship like Amy and Nina's is built on a history of consideration and respect. When a mother and daughter find themselves in a situation that neither considers ideal, it helps if they both have enough confidence in themselves and each other to discuss openly how to make the best of it. Amy and Nina's comfortable adjustment was easier because Nina didn't need to be the center of attention; she was as self-sufficient as her physical limitations allowed. And Amy didn't take advantage of her mother's dependence to try to make decisions for her—for example, by interfering with Nina's choice to try to hold on to her house when it seemed unlikely that she would be able to live there again.

When differences arise and everyone handles them as sensitively as Nina, Amy, and David did, the result is almost sure to be that a good relationship will get better, which it did.

Those who don't start with as well-balanced a relationship can take approaches that smooth out the tensions when adults live together, such as setting limits and negotiating as adults. But Grace and Mary Rose weren't able to do that. Without the techniques to set some house rules, they simply tried to love each other as best they could. Grace didn't fail her mother, but being a good daughter cost her a great deal, while Amy lost very little and gained a lot from her experience with a live-in mother.

CHAPTER 13

~

When Intimacy Is Elusive

Independent Mothers, Daughters Who Can't Get Close

A daughter is more likely to feel the weight of too much responsibility for her mother than too little. But highly independent mothers and women who have always been on the chilly side of the maternal spectrum can make their daughters feel extraneous in their lives as they age. It seems like a sort of rejection—and it often is—for a mother to push her daughter away just when other women have the opportunity for a last burst of intimacy with their mothers, even if working it out is painful and incomplete. Like daughters of abusive mothers, who must keep their distance to preserve their sanity, the daughters of mothers who are emotionally remote or who insist on doing everything themselves miss an important stage of interaction. Because cool mothers have often been underinvolved with their children all along, their daughters will add the loss of this last chance for closeness to a lifetime of disappointment and the feeling that they are only incidental in their mothers' lives.

For some mothers, the decline in independence can force at least a measure of intimacy. Whatever their personalities, many older women are not able to avoid outside assistance, either because their health is poor or their financial resources are inadequate. Even women who have always been paid for their work and are accustomed to being in control of their lives can find themselves on the brink of poverty as they age. (Remember that nearly 60 percent of women over seventy-five have incomes under ten thousand dollars a year.) When a rigidly independent mother begins to need help, neither she nor her daughter is likely to be prepared, and the lurch into another gear can send both mother and daughter jouncing around like passengers on a rutted road.

But when a mother truly *is* independent and is likely to stay that way, as Lynn's mother, Cynthia, is, the barrier between them may really be insurmountable. Cynthia hasn't yet encountered a practical situation she can't handle on her own, and she has set up her life so that she probably never will. Lynn has mourned her mother's "absence" all her life. Now that Cynthia is in her early eighties, Lynn's feeling of loss has been reactivated because she has so little time left to get her mother's attention.

⁓

LYNN AND CYNTHIA

"My mother has made it quite clear that she doesn't need me."

Lynn stopped by her publisher's office to pick up the first copy of the book about Renaissance painting she had written so she could take it with her when she went back to the Midwest to see her mother. "When I got to the farm, Mother was on her way out the door, but I couldn't wait. I pulled the book out of my bag and showed it to her. She didn't even look at it; she just said, 'Leave it on the table; I'm late for a meeting,' and off she went," Lynn says.

Cynthia had just bought a shiny new pickup truck, and Lynn stood in the doorway and watched her eighty-two-year-old mother haul herself up into the driver's seat and zoom down the drive. "You should have seen the dust cloud that truck left," Lynn says.

Lynn went upstairs to her old room and unpacked, got herself a glass of lemonade, and sat on the front porch, looking out over the fields and waiting for Cynthia to come home. "It was so hot I didn't even go down to the barn, which is usually my first stop," she says. "But when my mother got back, she looked as cool as though it were November. Even the weather can't get to her. The book was still on the front hall table, but Mother never glanced at it; she said, 'Dinner's at seven, as always,' went into her office, and closed the door."

The book stayed there, untouched, so when Lynn's brother arrived from California the next day and her sister, Priscilla, who lives in her own house on the farm, came for dinner, Lynn brought her book into the dining room to show them. "My mother said, 'You know we don't read at the table; we'll look at it later.' So I put it under my chair. I was there for a week; I moved the book around, putting it in places where she couldn't miss it, like her desk. I don't know if she ever opened it, but she never said anything, not even to acknowledge that I dedicated it to her," Lynn says.

"She didn't ignore it to be mean; she just had more important things to do. A couple of years before that, when she turned eighty, I asked her how it felt and she said, 'Not much time, and so much to accomplish.' That's as close to a personal conversation as we ever have. I keep trying, but she's not exactly introspective, and she doesn't want to hear what her children are thinking about or what we're doing. She has devoted the past thirty years to politics, community affairs, and the farm, and she just isn't very interested in anything else, including her children, grandchildren, or great-grandchildren.

"Even on our birthdays, all she does is send a card. She told us once, 'Don't expect me to remember your children's birthdays. Keeping track of yours is hard enough.' Since I was born on the same day she was, I'm not quite sure why it would be difficult, but I guess she was just making a point."

Lynn admits, "I shouldn't worry about being a 'good daughter' to my mother; she has made it clear that she doesn't need me. But what if she gets sick and can't do so much? I don't think she knows how to let anyone help her, and I doubt that she wants to learn."

Cynthia graduated from an eastern women's college in the 1930s. That summer, her father, a midwestern industrialist, sent her to Europe. She was already engaged to a young lawyer from her hometown and planned to be married the following spring. While she was away, her college chemistry professor wrote to offer her a job she had applied for, doing research at a distinguished university. Her father opened the letter and, without waiting to discuss it with Cynthia, answered it. "He wrote the professor that his daughter didn't need to work and that she was to be married," Lynn says. "You know when I learned that? *Last Christmas*, practically sixty years later, when I was up in my mother's attic looking for some old children's books to give to my granddaughter. I saw a set of chemistry slides and I didn't know what they were, so I asked Mother, and that's when she told me that she had hoped to have a research career. But she says after her father wrote that letter, she put the idea away, and she never thought about chemistry again."

Cynthia married Lynn's father, Andrew, as planned, and they moved out to the farm where Cynthia still lives. Andrew practiced small-town law, often taking on cases for free when a client couldn't afford to pay him. Lynn, their first child, was born when Cynthia was twenty-three. Lynn was four when her sister, Priscilla, was born. Cynthia promptly sent Lynn to live in town with Andrew's mother. "That was great, in a way," Lynn says, "because I really loved my grandmother. I stayed with her for three years, and then I went back home, to the farm. By then, my brother had been born, too, but my parents had more help, so I guess Mother felt that she could handle more than one child at a time. Our cook was the one who really brought us up. No one ever talked to me about why I lived with Granny or why I moved back home, although when I had my first child, my mother told me she had never liked babies or even little children."

Cynthia and Andrew were farmers; they were also the children of Victorian parents and their household was formal and traditional. They had high standards of behavior and accomplishment for themselves and their children. "We were supposed to be naturally good at everything," Lynn says, "so when I took ballet lessons and I was sort of clumsy, I used to go out to the barn to practice. I didn't want my mother to know that it didn't come easily to me. It wasn't hard to keep secrets from her; she was more like a family manager than a mother. I don't think she has much maternal instinct.

"My best childhood memories are of the times my mother and I did things together: riding, fishing, playing tennis. We never had the kind of cozy, sit-around-the-kitchen-table chats other mothers and daughters have. The only time she ever showed emotion was when I was a teenager and we had colossal fights—which Mother won.

"If you have a parent like that, you have to find a refuge. Mine was books. I went away to boarding school when I was twelve—I was two years younger than the oldest girl in my class. By the time I was nineteen, I was a senior in college. But it didn't matter how well I did in school, I always had the feeling that Mother didn't quite notice me."

During Lynn's senior year, her father was killed in a farming accident. "From the minute he died, my mother never talked about him again or about the accident. She had him buried immediately—none of us children even knew where—and then held a memorial service. I found out where my father's grave is only two or three years ago. My brother was riding on the farm and found his gravestone. He came home and asked my mother why she had been so secretive. She said, 'It's best to put some things behind you. What good would talking about it have done?'"

A couple of months after her father's death, over Lynn's spring vacation, she announced to her mother that she had decided to get married. Although Lynn had just turned twenty and Cynthia had never met the young man, the only questions she asked had to do with his pedigree: What did his father do? Was his a "good" family? When the answers were satisfactory, Cynthia's reaction was to take out her telephone book and start making a list of guests to invite to the wedding. "She just took over," Lynn says, "and did what she does best: make arrangements." Lynn was married a week after graduation.

Cynthia hadn't been widowed for long when she launched her second attempt at a career; this time there wasn't anyone who could stop her. Andrew had left her well enough off so she didn't need to earn a salary, and she had always been involved in community affairs, so she decided to run for the state legislature. Cynthia won the first time out, served for twenty years, and became state cochair of her political party.

Lynn had started a career, too, as an art historian at a museum. Her personal life wasn't going as well; she was taking care of her first child and divorcing her husband. "Mother was always good when there was a problem," Lynn says. "You knew you could count on her to be sensible and organized, but her idea of a crisis wasn't always the same as anyone else's." Lynn's divorce didn't seem like crisis material to Cynthia. "She was completely unsympathetic, but at least she wasn't critical," Lynn says. "A long time later, I asked her why she didn't think it was a big deal. She said, 'Oh, I knew you'd get married again.'"

Lynn did remarry and had two more children. Her own style of mothering was warm, although, she admits, "My household was kind of bohemian. I guess I felt that by being wild and free, at least I'd get a reaction. But it didn't matter what I did; Mother was busy, and she simply didn't notice."

Priscilla, Lynn's younger sister, took the opposite approach to get Cynthia's attention. She modeled herself after her mother, married a local lawyer, moved into a house on the farm, and picked her own area of public service in which to make her career. Cynthia's principal interests have been in preserving the integrity and economy of the state's villages; the main square in the town near her farm is named for her. Priscilla focused on environmental issues and was eventually appointed director of a state agency. "Mother didn't seem any more interested in what Priscilla was doing than she was in my life," Lynn says. "When Priscilla was sworn in, Mother declared that she was too busy to attend. It didn't matter if you were the bad girl or the good girl, if you weren't a civic cause, you weren't worthy of much regard."

Lynn's brother, Andy, didn't try as hard to please his mother; he went his own way—west. He attended college and medical school in California and is now a surgeon in Los Angeles. Andy and Lynn coordinate their visits to Cynthia to be there at the same time. "It helps to have him around when I have to face my mother and I'm reminded that she never seems to be seeing us straight on; it's as though she just catches a glimpse of us out of the corner of her eye, while her attention is focused on something more important," Lynn says.

Lynn is not particularly concerned about the practical aspects of her mother's old age. Cynthia has already identified an assisted-living community she would move to if she can no longer live at the farm. She has made extensive, detailed plans for her funeral and ordered her gravestone.

What does worry Lynn is that, with everything arranged just the way her mother wants it, there may never be a time when Cynthia is open or vulnerable enough for Lynn to slip through a crack and connect more intimately with her or show her what a good daughter she can be. "I'd like, just once, for her to need me; I'd like her to see that I can handle a tough situation, too," Lynn says, "and I wish she could let a little bit of love leak out into the open. I've tried to get her to be more demonstrative by telling her I love her, but she just says, 'Don't get all mushy on me.'

"So you know what I do? I figure I've got a lot of love to hand out. I give it where it's welcome, to my own children and grandchildren, but I still hope that someday I'll troll a little love by my mother, and she'll take the bait."

Accepting What You Can't Change

Cynthia doesn't need her children to take care of her in her old age. She is busy and useful, healthy, sociable, and financially independent. So what is the problem? Even daughters who have no real responsibility for aging mothers feel as though in this last stage a particular kind of closeness is called for, a final opportunity for a mother and daughter to become friends as adults and perhaps to redress what went wrong between them. But Cynthia is not comfortable with intimacy, and what has been "wrong" between her and her children is that they can't get close to her. She is shut down tight, and it seems that she will never permit any of her children the friendship and remediation they would like. She doesn't even acknowledge their accomplishments, which is an important element in establishing mature interdependence.

Lynn and Priscilla can't stop comparing themselves to their successful mother and feeling inadequate because she overlooks their own significant achievements. Lynn goes back again and again—and Priscilla has never really left—to seek recognition. In Cynthia's obliviousness to her daughters' successes, she is similar to Mary Rose, who never acknowledged Grace's strengths. And, like Grace, Lynn and Priscilla have shaped much of their lives in an effort to get the recognition their mother is evidently incapable of giving them. Yet Grace, at least, was able to do things for her mother and feel as though she had been a good daughter. Lynn and Priscilla are unlikely to have that opportunity.

Lynn's decision to compensate for the dearth of love from her mother by loving her own children and grandchildren the way she wishes she had been loved is a healthy way to show herself that she doesn't have to be like Cynthia. And by redirecting her attention to being a loving mother and grandmother, Lynn has brought herself into the orbit of an affectionate family circle, even though her mother chooses to remain on its outskirts.

If Lynn can simply admire her mother the way so many people who are *not* Cynthia's children do—as a remarkable woman dedicated to community service, who gives considerably more than she asks for, at least in the public arena—Cynthia's last years will be easier for both of them. Cynthia has shown her children that independence and control are of primary importance to her. Lynn's greatest service to her mother will be to take particular care not to undermine Cynthia's strengths and to let her handle her old age on her own, the way she wants to.

Facing what your mother can and can't do is part of the process of letting go of the flawless imaginary mother who inhabits the dreams of children. Alas, that fictional mother still lurks, in her apron or her party dress, smelling of whatever each of us thinks a mother should smell of—hot apple cider and fresh-baked cookies or a glamorous perfume that represents the world of grown-ups that looked so magical from the outside. Adults learn to accept each other's failings, but inside each adult is the memory of the child who wants her mother to match some ideal and aches with longing when she can't change her. Part of being a good daughter is to accept our mothers as they are and love them despite their imperfections—the way a good mother loves her children.

~

JESSICA AND WILLA

"How am I supposed to help her if she insists on retaining control, even after she dies?"

Not every highly independent mother has the same choices Cynthia does. She doesn't have any financial worries, her health and independence are uncompromised, and even if she becomes disabled and can't live on her own, her detailed plans will enable her to continue to feel in control of her own destiny. Other women who have always worked and are accustomed to being in control of their own lives are not as lucky. Even if they have been financially prudent, a protracted old age can not only devour whatever money they may have been able to put aside but can also threaten their children's financial stability if they have to help support their mothers.

Financial insecurity raises troubling emotional as well as practical issues, both for an elderly woman who is used to being self-sufficient and for her daughter. Women of our mother's generation who worked conveyed a special competence because they were exceptions to the norm. A daughter who has been accustomed to believing that her mother can combine family and work and take care of herself and others may be unprepared for the way she will feel when her mother becomes dependent.

And like Jessica, whose mother, Willa, is still working at eighty-four, a daughter whose mother has always acted as though she doesn't trust her daughter to be as competent as she is may not feel qualified to take a more active role as caretaker when it becomes necessary.

When Jessica was five, Willa started her career as a saleswoman in a department store. She was promoted to buyer and eventually became the manager of a merchandise category. She loves working and she is still employed, but the current phase of her career is not one she would necessarily have chosen.

Jessica, the older of Willa's two daughters, is divorced, with no children of her own. Her younger sister has serious psychological problems and is living on disability insurance, and Jessica is the child on whom Willa would count—if Willa were willing to count on anyone. "My mother thinks she is the only one who can do anything right," Jessica says. "I have a good job, certainly as good as the best job my mother ever had, but Ma still thinks I'm totally incompetent."

Meanwhile, the otherwise extremely competent Willa made a serious mistake that has undermined her financial security. Her savings are gone. Her bank account is empty by the end of each month. And if Jessica has to contribute to Willa's support, it could jeopardize Jessica's future by depleting the meager fund she has been able to build for her own old age.

"After my father died, my mother married again," Jessica explains. "It was okay for a couple of years, until her new husband decided he wanted to retire. 'Fine,' my mother said. 'You can stay home; I'm going to work.' But he wanted her hanging around, making lunch for him, and entertaining him all day. He started to do weird things while she was at work, like breaking her china and hiding the pieces in strange places, and he got really abusive. So my mother said, 'This has got to stop. I'm divorcing him.' To get rid of him, she gave him the house my father left her, which was the capital she was supposed to have for her old age. I begged her not to do it, but she wouldn't listen.

"Ma moved to Florida, where she thought she could live on her pension and Social Security, but it was more expensive there than she had expected. It's hard to believe this, but she went out and got herself another job. By then she was in her late seventies, but she lied about her age and got away with it. Even now, at eighty-four, she still looks like she's in her sixties. She's selling real estate on commission, so I guess it's not like a salaried job with benefits, where you have to tell them your real age.

"But the real estate market isn't very good, and she's hardly earning any money. And what if she gets sick and can't work at all? Last year, she had a lumpectomy, which she didn't tell me about. Then she came to visit me in Chicago, where I live, and mentioned, like it was no big deal, that she'd had the procedure. 'What did they find?' I asked her. 'Nothing worth talking about,' she said."

Then when Willa returned to Florida, she called Jessica and said she had breast cancer and was going into the hospital to have a mastectomy. "Ma! Why didn't you tell me when you were here?" Jessica said.

"I didn't want to ruin the trip," Willa answered.

Jessica took time off from work and immediately flew to Florida to be with her mother for the operation. "I got there a couple of days early, and she took me into her bedroom and showed me her living will, which she had taped to the wall; her safe, which she had left open because she was afraid that I wouldn't be able to remember the combination; and a list of everyone I was to call if she died. She had also made up a kit with a multitude of forms in it, all filled out, for her funeral arrangements. That was so if she died during surgery, I, the incompetent, wouldn't have to make any decisions. How am I supposed to help her if she insists on retaining control, even after she dies?"

When the operation was over and Willa was recovering, Jessica told her never to keep a health problem a secret from her again. She said if Willa told her she was fine, she wouldn't know whether to believe her, and she refused to worry all the time that her mother was lying about her health. "I think it worked," Jessica says. "As far as I can tell, she hasn't lied to me since."

After her illness, Willa was also more open to discussing the future with her daughter. She agreed to Jessica's suggestion that, while she was there, she could research the public and private social services that might be available if Willa came to need them. Then, together, they could figure out the options and costs and make some contingency plans.

Speaking up and taking responsibility helped Jessica feel like a better daughter. Her initiative in helping her mother sort out the future has also given her more confidence, and their relationship has become less lopsided. Now Jessica doesn't feel as resentful that Willa didn't have a more realistic sense of self-preservation, which may have prevented her financial problems.

It is particularly difficult for Jessica to see how unsteadily her mother occupies the pedestal she erected for herself. To Jessica, her mother was, above all, an independent woman. When Jessica compared herself to her mother, she always came out behind, and, rather than seeing Willa as a role model, she felt there was nothing she could do to match her in competence. Even when Jessica's judgment was better than Willa's—for example, when Willa decided to give her house away to get rid of her second husband—Jessica felt too much like a little girl to do more than beg her to reconsider.

Willa's vulnerability gave Jessica a way to be part of her mother's life. After seeing how unprepared Willa is for the problems that are beginning to encroach on her independence, Jessica began to be more realistic—to grow up, in a sense—and take a more aggressive role in planning for her own old age. Jessica recognizes that Willa's impatience to solve a problem immediately and move on worked only as long as Willa could keep earning money. So Jessica is determined to be more competent than her mother by making long-term plans. She has met with an advisor who is helping her develop a savings and investment program and has figured out how much money she will need to set aside to supplement her own pension and Social Security. Jessica still admires her mother's gumption and ability, but she has finally been able to see that Willa isn't invulnerable and that, by comparison, Jessica isn't "the incompetent one."

Mothers who are independent, either by disposition or because of their financial circumstances, are in some ways like the self-sufficient women of the baby boom generation. Yet, as Cynthia and Willa illustrate, a mother who is successfully engaged in the world beyond her family and has more in common with similarly occupied daughters is not necessarily easier to be close to than a less worldly mother.

An appropriate way to be a good daughter to an independent mother is to try not to interfere with her determination to lead her life the way she always has and to be sensitive to her fear of losing her effectiveness in the community or in business. (For younger women who plan to work until they either are forcibly retired or die at their desks, it is useful to keep in mind that when we age, our daughters, too, may hope that we will become more accessible. Perhaps, then, we will find a way to put our work into better perspective and open up a little extra space for closeness.)

One of the empty places in distant mother-daughter relationships is the passing along of knowledge, understanding, and a model for the future. A woman in the middle of her life knows how fast the last thirty years have gone by, and she can hardly ignore the fact that the next few decades will race past as well. Women like Cynthia and Willa, who are not in any stereotypically way "old," show that age and decline are not inevitably linked, and that is a substantial contribution. But their daughters would also like the benefit of their insights about this rushing passage of time. Have their mothers made their peace with it, or do they just refuse to consider it, the way Cynthia refused to think about her husband's death? Cynthia and Willa are like many members of their generation in their unwillingness to talk about personal matters and deep feelings. Even women who are close to their mothers often learn more about age and mortality from observing their mothers than from anything they say.

CHAPTER 14

⁓

Long-Distance Daughters,
Unresolved Issues

Logistics and Feelings

No single issue or circumstance can describe a relationship. Emotional difficulties and practical issues get snarled together and complicate each other. One situation that makes it hard to sort out feelings and logistics is when a mother and daughter live far apart. Long-distance relationships diminish the opportunities to work out unresolved issues—although distance can enable some mothers and daughters to develop perspective about themselves and each other.

Geographic separation has many drawbacks. It is harder for a daughter to be responsible when she lives thousands of miles from her mother, it is only sporadically possible to be companionable, and when a mother and daughter don't see each other often, even their love for each other can seem rather abstract.

Daughters tend to resist admitting that the once-powerful mothers they remember are waning, even if some of their power was misused and their interactions have often been unpleasant. But it is even harder to let go of the familiar mother figure a daughter has installed in her memory if mothers and daughters don't spend enough time together as adults for them to develop new patterns.

The relationship between Isabelle and her mother, Frances, was marked—almost defined—by a long and acrimonious history of competition over which of them was more attractive, dressed better, was smarter, or had a nicer house. But for many years, they lived on separate coasts and got together only a couple of times a year, so their old competition seemed to have been subdued. When Isabelle had to take a more active role in her mother's care, however, her evaluation of the options about where Frances should live was confused by old feelings that obscured the current realities.

~

FRANCES AND ISABELLE

"You look so good in everything and I'm so fat. You don't know how it feels to be old."

Frances and Isabelle had the "dressing room episode" just after Frances turned eighty. "We went shopping together, which we've always loved to do," Isabelle says. "Appearance is very important to my mother. I was the best-dressed girl in school. My mother still happily tells stories about the poodle skirt she made for me or how she bought me my first ball gown and bronze sandals to match. We were both 'fashion animals'—even though a big part of that equation was Mother's insistence that her taste was better than mine and that I needed her advice if I wanted to look chic." So when Frances came to visit Isabelle, the two women did what they had always done together: they set off to look for clothes.

"I was in the dressing room," Isabelle says, "and my mother was waiting for me out in the department. She hadn't found anything she liked, but I had brought in three suits to try on—it was one of those days when you find what you want fast. I was in my underwear when I heard her sobbing. So I threw on my clothes and ran out there. Mother was sitting in a chair, and a couple of saleswomen were bending over her and trying to comfort her. Mother looked up at me and said, 'You look good in everything and I'm so fat. You don't know how it feels to be old.'"

Isabelle left the store without buying anything, drove her mother back to her house, where she was staying, and went to her office. "I was incredibly relieved to be at work," she says, "away from my mother and her tantrums. But I realized that part of the reason I was so upset was that I knew that one of the things we had shared was over. We would never go shopping together again. It felt like a big loss to me, but what my mother had lost was infinitely worse."

Fashion served as a bond between Frances and Isabelle, but competition gave their common interest in clothes a sharp edge. When Isabelle was a teenager her mother's envy of her looks began to emerge. Before appearance became an issue between them, Frances's sore spot was her daughter's intelligence. Isabelle says her mother was "charming, sociable, and loving"; ran a "warm, if messy" suburban household; loved to give parties; and was a volunteer at the local historical society, which in the Virginia city where they lived was an interesting and prestigious organization. But Frances was insecure about her intellect, a feeling that was exacerbated by her husband. "Mother was deferential and fearful around Dad and she walked on eggshells when he was home," Isabelle says. "He was handsome, dashing, and very smart. But when he was drinking, which was often, he ridiculed my mother and made her feel stupid. Mother reacted by affecting a superficial disinterest in anything intellectual."

When Isabelle was three, Frances decided that her daughter was "brilliant," like her father. "Mother announced that I was too much for her to handle and I was giving her a nervous breakdown," Isabelle says. "Great lesson: if you're too smart, you'll drive your mother crazy." Frances's doctor advised her to send Isabelle to school full-time, since she couldn't cope, so Isabelle's academic career started earlier than most children's did during the late 1940s.

Isabelle is the oldest of three children; her younger siblings were both male, and her mother used to say, "One girl is harder than two boys." When Isabelle was ready to go to high school, Frances announced, "Isabelle is so smart she can go to the public high school," although her brothers both went to private schools.

Rather than admiring her academic endeavors, Isabelle says, "Mother was more interested in what boys I was going out with. She encouraged my 'female side.'" Much of that encouragement was centered on Isabelle's appearance, but as Isabelle entered adolescence, Frances began to make comparisons between them, and Frances didn't like the way she came out. Isabelle was tall, slim, and blond; Frances was shorter, dark-haired, and more solidly built. "My mother was always a little jealous of me," Isabelle says, "and it got worse and worse. When I was in high school, she started to borrow my clothes, even though they didn't fit her. Then she wouldn't give them back. She seemed to think she could look like me if she wore what I wore, even though she was very critical of my taste.

"Mother was always very interested in who I was dating because she saw men as saviors," Isabelle continues, "so I rebelled. In high school, I went out with tough guys from the 'wrong' families. That drove her crazy, too." Then, when Isabelle graduated from college, she became engaged to her first husband, Ben. Frances was delighted. Ben came from a respected family, worked for a manufacturing firm started by his grandfather, and was well-off. But Frances's pleasure was soon curdled by jealousy. When Isabelle and Ben moved into a house that was as nice as Frances's house, "My mother started to go on about how my life was better than hers," Isabelle says. "She'd invite me out to tea, then make me pay. Or she'd come over to visit and see something she liked—it could have been anything, soap in the guest bathroom or a sweater—and she would ask for it. Then she would turn around and do the same old thing: tell me I wasn't quite up to the mark in the taste department. I remember one time when I bought a big bunch of pink carnations—I love their spicy smell, and they're not expensive, so you can get a lot of them and make a big arrangement—and Mother said they were 'middle-class flowers'. Can you imagine? A couple of years ago, I read that one of the French couture designers loved carnations and had them all over his house. I clipped the article and sent it to my mother, still trying to prove that I was right."

Isabelle and Ben had two sons. After the younger boy was born, Isabelle began to teach at a local private school and to take night courses to get her master's degree in English. She and Ben started to feel they had less and less in common, and when their sons were small, they decided to move to California to make a new start. After a couple of years, they realized they couldn't restore their relationship and divorced.

Isabelle and her children moved back across the country to Virginia. Isabelle's father had died a few years earlier, and Frances suggested that Isabelle and the boys stay with her while Isabelle went back to graduate school to get her doctorate.

"Mother was very keen for me to move in with her but angry with me for leaving my husband, whom she loved and is still close to," Isabelle says. "She started to punish me. First she didn't let me use her car, so my uncle lent me a car. Then I set up my office in her big living room. No one ever went in there, but she said I was in the way, and she banished me to the attic, which was unheated in the winter and stifling in the summer.

"She expected me to entertain her; she thought graduate school was just a way to amuse myself. She told me I was neurotic because I worked so hard—that was part of her old insecurity about intelligence. The competition about looks was still there, too. When I started dating again and a man invited me to a black-tie party, I discovered that my mother had given all my dressy clothes to the school theater department. She said they were out of style."

At that point, Isabelle was looking for a job and had very little money. She didn't ask her mother for financial help, and Ben paid part of his child support to Frances as rent, but Frances began to complain about how much it cost to keep Isabelle and her sons in the house. "Mother actually told me I should be on welfare, although there was no way I qualified," Isabelle says. "She kept saying I should never have left my husband. I think the idea that I was poor confirmed her opinion that I had made bad decisions."

Isabelle's best job offer was at a book-publishing company in California. By then, her sons were both away at college, so Isabelle moved out of Frances's house and went back to the West Coast, where she met and married her second husband.

For the next ten years, Frances and Isabelle saw each other only a few times a year. "Our visits were difficult until I finally told her she shouldn't give me advice or criticize me," Isabelle says. "She said, 'I'm just being a mother.' But I said, 'I'm too old for that kind of mother. It's time for you to make the transition to being another adult family member. You don't get to have an administrative or advisory role anymore.' She accepted that. I would ask her advice only about a recipe or a china pattern or something about the family: straight information."

Until their unfortunate shopping expedition, Frances and Isabelle had a reasonably comfortable long-distance friendship. But shortly after that visit, Frances's life fell apart. Frances was in her early eighties when her elder son, John, the child Frances was closest to, died. Isabelle went back to Virginia for the funeral and stayed with Frances. When Isabelle came back into her mother's life in a more intensive way, the shadow of Frances's competition and criticism affected Isabelle's ability to see her situation objectively.

Isabelle could tell right away that her mother was different, but she told herself that Frances's behavior was a side effect of grief that would probably abate when she began to adjust to John's death. "Mother was forgetful and uncoordinated; she couldn't put the phone on the hook the right way," Isabelle says. "She was lost without John. I didn't realize that she'd stopped driving, because John always drove her. He managed her accounts, he fixed things in the house, and he and his wife went to Mother's every Sunday for lunch."

Isabelle took a month's leave from her job so she and her younger brother, who lived an hour away from Frances, could sort out what kind of help Frances needed to fill at least part of the hole John's death had left in her life. Frances had never been a particularly good housekeeper, so Isabelle and her brother spent much of the next couple of weeks cleaning her house and making it more functional. They bought her a new stove and refrigerator, mops and brooms, and a modern vacuum cleaner to replace the old upright model Frances had owned since the 1950s. They put up bulletin boards and posted important phone numbers on them. They brought in telephones with large touchpads and big numbers.

The house didn't stay clean for long. Frances had two dogs, one of whom was a huge and ancient Labrador retriever with ulcerated sores on his legs and such bad arthritis that he couldn't walk. He was too large to be carried outside, and he defecated and urinated in the kitchen, which soon began to smell bad again. The second dog, a small terrier mix, had begun to attack him, and Isabelle would hear the Lab crying in the night and find blood on the hallway floor downstairs. "The condition of the dogs was the biggest clue to the fact that Mother was losing her grip. I don't know why I continued to think she could take care of herself when she couldn't care for them; she had always been terrific with animals," Isabelle says.

Frances wanted to stay in her home, so Isabelle got in touch with social service organizations and arranged for someone to come in every morning to cook her lunch and stop back again in the evening to make sure she was all right. Frances resisted at first. "She was furious about the idea of having strangers in her house. She said we were taking over her life, bossing her around," Isabelle says, "which, of course, we were."

But Frances's children had good reason to think they might have to take responsibility for her. When Isabelle went back to California, Frances began to make late-night phone calls to her younger son, insisting that he come over because she heard noises. She started to "see" people in the house, too—a family having a picnic in her dining room or an old friend. Isabelle began to understand that Frances's condition might be more than a reaction to grief, and she called Frances's doctor, made an appointment, and, unwilling to ask her brother to handle alone what she feared would be bad news, Isabelle flew back to Virginia to go with her.

The doctor recommended that Frances check into the hospital for an assessment. When it became clear that the hospital stay would be prolonged, Isabelle returned to California and monitored the situation with her brother; they were now speaking on the phone every few days.

While Frances was in the hospital, her son took the ill and suffering Lab to the veterinarian to be put down and found a new home for the small dog, whose bad temper the vet attributed to the fact that Frances sometimes neglected to feed him. "I dreaded telling Mother about the dogs," Isabelle says. "I did it as gently as possible, but she barely reacted. It seemed like a sign that she was becoming detached from her old life."

Frances spent weeks in the hospital, undergoing tests and observations, but the doctors couldn't find out exactly what was wrong with her because her symptoms—some physical, some mental—came and went. The doctors said she wasn't well enough to go home, but, Isabelle says, "I was still sure she didn't need to be in a nursing home."

Isabelle flew back to Virginia—again—to look for an appropriate residential situation for Frances. By this time, Isabelle was getting behind on her work and beginning to worry that her boss would run out of patience if she continued to ask for time off.

In the search for a place where Frances could live, the intensity of their old competition about appearances resurfaced. "I thought Mother would want to be in a place that felt like her home, and where the other people were the sort she would want to socialize with," Isabelle says, "but even more, I was afraid that if I chose a place that wasn't filled with women wearing good wool suits and men in tweed sports jackets, Mother would launch into a tirade, like the ones I used to get when I went out with 'trashy' boys or bought carnations."

Isabelle located a residence in a big house on an old estate that had formally landscaped gardens and a gracefully designed new wing with sunny, ground-floor rooms. Because the property was now surrounded by housing developments, the cost of staying there wasn't too high. The other residents were well dressed and alert. "When I saw everyone gathering in the drawing room for cocktails, I called my brother and said, 'I've found it. If anything can restore Mother to her old self, this is it!'"

But what the residence offered in charm was not nearly

enough to cover Frances's needs. She had drifted considerably farther from her "old self" than her children were willing to recognize, and she required professional nursing and virtually full-time care. At the residence, her deterioration quickly became apparent. She didn't make friends, she was hostile to the staff, and she was confused; for example, she couldn't find the toilet handle in her bathroom. When Isabelle's brother took her out for lunch, she seemed lively and clearheaded—until she had to go to the bathroom, when she stood up from the table and began pulling down her underwear. Finally, Frances told the staff at the residence that she was pregnant, and Isabelle got "the call." The director explained that Frances needed more specialized care and would have to move again.

"I fooled myself into thinking Mother was better than she was," Isabelle says. "I couldn't let go of the stylish mother I knew, who loved attractive houses and people. And I couldn't take the risk that if the place I found wasn't up to her standards, she would use it as the final proof that I was a disappointment to her because my taste wasn't good enough. I chose a home for the person she used to be, the one I remembered. But that person had begun to fade a couple of years earlier; she was on her way out that day she had the crying fit in the department store."

Frances is now in a full-care nursing home. It is utilitarian rather than elegant, but it provides the services Frances needs, and Isabelle's brother has been monitoring the care at close range, sometimes dropping in without calling first to be sure his mother is clean and comfortable and to observe the way the staff treats patients. Isabelle went to visit Frances after she had been there for a few weeks and brought her a package of clothes. Frances was delighted with the gift, but she thought someone else had sent it. "I was upset by the way my mother looked. She's being well cared for, but she looks disheveled and small, like a caricature of a little old lady. Still, I'll keep buying her clothes to comfort myself," Isabelle says.

The medications Frances is taking calm her anxiety. Although she is disoriented some of the time, she has become softer and more affectionate. "Mother doesn't seem unhappy, and when I visit her or talk to her on the phone, I'm relieved to hear that she hasn't completely lost her sense of humor," Isabelle says. "But she's slipping into the gray area now; she is so powerless and alone, and her life has changed so much. I have a lot of empathy for her. Perhaps it's partly because she doesn't have the power to compete with me anymore, but I feel and act more lovingly toward her than I ever could before."

Finding the "Real" Mother

Isabelle's story reflects the complexity of being a good daughter to an aging mother; and how the many ingredients we have to measure and mix can make life confusing. For Isabelle, long-distance daughtering was combined with unresolved appearance issues, lack of communication, the gap between her life and her mother's, and Frances's poor health. Hardly any of these problems lend themselves to being definitively solved.

Isabelle's instinctual desire to place her failing mother in an inappropriate residential facility is a common mistake. Her decision was based on her image of her mother and on her need to please her, which overwhelmed her ability to recognize the services Frances needed. Although even professionals can have a hard time diagnosing the severity of symptoms such as Frances had, a family member's appraisal can be clouded by the tendency to hold on to both the good and bad aspects of a mother's personality, even when she is obviously impaired.

Frances and Isabelle's shared interest in appearance, mixed with the competition Frances felt toward her daughter, fed into Isabelle's miscalculation. So much of their connection had centered on the way they and their surroundings looked that it was hard for Isabelle to let go of that aspect of her mother. When Frances wasn't well enough to live in a place that met her old standards, Isabelle rightly understood that to be a symbol that she was losing her "real" mother.

The fact that they lived three thousand miles apart and Isabelle couldn't personally monitor the situation made her even more anxious to be sure her mother was in the "right" place. She felt guilty because she couldn't see her mother regularly so she overcompensated by finding a residence that provided a gracious environment and a social life of the sort that had always been important to Frances.

When Isabelle realized that Frances had changed and that the competition between them was over, at last she was able to feel more love and empathy for her.

~⌐

SUSAN AND BARBARA

"I hated my mother, so I moved as far away from her as I could."

The desire to fit our lives into cohesive stories—so we can package them and continue on our way without being tripped by loose ends—can be an underlying reason for a daughter to create a substantial geographic distance between her and her mother. A daughter who decides that she can thrive only if she lives far away from her mother may be right, but she may also have created new obstacles that will surface when her mother is old.

Susan, a university professor, spent most of her adult life putting as much distance between herself and her mother, Barbara, as she could. The reason she gave was a flat "I hated my mother, and she hated me." But when Barbara had been dead a few years and Susan began to replay their relationship in her mind, she realized that she had oversimplified and that she and her mother could have been better friends if Susan had been able to develop more perspective.

A lot of the problems between them were played out in the arena of appearance. Barbara weighed 210 pounds when she married Susan's father. Then he went to fight in World War II. When he came back, Barbara was down to 145.

"To maintain her weight, or go lower, she became an alcoholic," Susan says. "She smoked all day instead of eating, and around four o'clock, when the hunger pangs were too strong, she'd have her first drink. By dinner, when she finally ate a normal meal, she was drunk."

Barbara's insecurity influenced her attitude toward Susan from the time she was born. "The mythology was that I was so homely that when my grandmother came to see me in the hospital, she said, 'That can't be our baby; she's too ugly,'" Susan reports. "That's what my mother told me, anyway."

Actually, Susan was an adorable child who grew up to be a very pretty teenager. She had silky, pale blond hair; a long, lean body; great posture; and lovely skin. "But my mother always made fun of my 'chicken hair,'" Susan says. "You can imagine how I felt about the way I looked when I went to dancing class with boys. I was about twelve. My mother was so worried that I wouldn't be popular that she used to give me one of her diet pills to get me 'up.'"

Susan dealt with what felt like her mother's disgust that she had an ugly duckling daughter by deciding that she and her mother hated each other. When she talked about Barbara, though, she also mentioned stories about her mother's good side.

During her sophomore year in college, Susan thought she was pregnant. She urgently insisted that Barbara come to Boston to pick her up at the end of the semester, but she refused to tell her why. Barbara didn't press her—she just got into her car on the appointed day and drove to Susan's school. When Barbara got there, Susan was so embarrassed she made her guess what was wrong. Finally, Susan says, "I blurted it out."

Barbara didn't criticize Susan; instead she went directly to the practical questions. Did Susan want the baby? And if she didn't—this was in the early 1960s—what could they do about it?

Susan wasn't pregnant after all. "But one good thing I can say about my mother is that she was great in a crisis," she says, and she proceeds to talk about other times her mother proved to be a staunch ally.

Yet Susan continued to feel that Barbara was a threat to her self-confidence, so she went to graduate school on the West Coast, never lived in the East again, and saw Barbara only two or three times a year after that. By the time Barbara was widowed and living in Florida, Susan was teaching at a university in Hawaii.

Then Barbara developed acute emphysema. As the disease progressed into its final phase, Barbara, who had only 12 percent of her lung capacity, was hospitalized, and Susan flew back to be with her.

Although Barbara had a living will, she had been put on life support. When Susan arrived at the hospital, she found that her mother's arms were in restraints because she had pulled out the breathing apparatus twice. In Florida, to take someone off life support, the agreement of three doctors was required. So Susan set out to see Barbara's doctors and get them to accede to her request to remove the tubes and let Barbara live the way she wanted in her last weeks. The first doctor told her that Barbara's heart was strong and asked why Susan was "in such a hurry." The second said that Susan stood to inherit from her mother and so he could not agree to her request. If Susan had been in closer contact with her mother, she might have had enough of a relationship with the doctors to have earned their confidence. Instead, she watched her mother struggle, unable to speak because of the tubes in her throat.

As Barbara held on to life week after week, Susan had to go back to Hawaii to teach, while an aunt came to keep Barbara company at the hospital. Barbara died shortly after Susan left. "She was sitting up, looking out the window, with those damn tubes in her, unable to say good-bye or tell us she loved us," Susan says, her blue eyes magnified by tears. Then she adds, "I guess I didn't hate her after all."

Susan and Isabelle both chose to lead much of their adult lives out of range of their mothers. Other women, whose mothers are competitive, intrusive, critical, or demanding—or display any of the range of traits that can interfere with an adult daughter's ability to get on with her life—make the same choices. They, too, must be wary of the consequences of avoiding regular contact and losing the opportunity to mend their differences before their mothers die.

What of women who wish they could live near their mothers but have had to move because of their jobs or their husbands' work? Many of them also struggle with feelings they might have outgrown if they and their mothers had been able to use the skills most people develop as they mature. The disjunction between the past and the present that can be a side effect of a long-distance relationship feels a bit like going to a thirtieth high school reunion. You may now be the most successful member of the class and have a happy marriage and children who are stars themselves, but it doesn't take long to drop back into the style of the girl you once were—the most or least popular, the brain, the ditz, or the jock. If you and your classmates had been together as you all evolved, you would eventually have cast off your outgrown roles to see each other as the adults you have become.

A daughter who doesn't spend enough time with her mother so their relationship can develop past the pubescent stage can still remind herself that she is no longer the girl who fought so bitterly for a later curfew, that she can now come home at any hour she chooses, and that she can let down her guard and treat her mother like a friend instead of the enemy whose rules she once fought to overturn. In response, when she and her mother do see each other, her mother may also treat her like an adult and recognize her accomplishments rather than reacting to the outdated remnants of her teenage rebellion.

Loss

Roseanne Beard with her three sons, Anson, standing, Peter, left, and my former husband, Sam, right, early 1940s. The last time I saw my mother-in-law before she died, we spent a wonderful evening together, looking through her photograph albums. Reviewing old pictures and talking about the past is a form of "life review" that is satisfying both to older people and to their children and grandchildren. But seeing pictures of your mother (or in this case, mother-in-law) as she was when she was young is also a poignant reminder of how inexorably time passes.

PART III

Loss

CHAPTER 15

~

The Last Chapter

When we were young, before we loved our husbands and children, most of us loved and trusted our mothers in a way we rarely experience again after childhood. The death of a mother seemed like an insuperable calamity that would place us in great jeopardy and blight our lives forever.

It is not coincidental that many of the tragic heroines we read about as children—Snow White, Cinderella, Heidi, Sarah Crewe, Jane Eyre—had misadventures that were precipitated by the fact that their mothers weren't around to protect them. If there were fathers in these stories, they tended to be dangerously dense. Look what happened to Sarah Crewe, the Little Princess: her father went off to war and left her with a mean schoolmistress whose flattering manner would never have passed the good-mother test of authenticity. Cinderella's father didn't even notice that her wicked stepmother and stepsisters had turned her into a scullery maid, and Snow White's father was a king, yet he couldn't protect her from his jeal-

215

ous wife, the stepmother who sent Snow White off to be murdered. A good mother would never let such things happen to her daughter.

Now that we are grown and the death of our mothers is considerably more imminent, our emotions are not as simple as they were when we felt we needed them to survive. Now they need us, an inversion that our instincts tell us is unnatural. When we add our mothers' dependence to the residue of our fears that they will smother, neglect, or disapprove of us, sometimes the prospect of their death seems like a relief—but only briefly. Then the whole thing flips over, and we feel like children again, as though we will be undefended once our mothers are gone. We mourn them in advance; we still grieve for them long after they have died. (Occasionally, my own mother refers to herself as an orphan, even though she understands that not many women her age have living parents. Just in case she has forgotten, I remind her that if my grandmother were still alive, she would be 106, a number that, if it were a fever, would be borderline fatal.)

We grieve for ourselves, too, as we muddle our mothers' last illnesses and deaths with our own vulnerability and mortality. But just as we have learned from our mothers' examples before—what to do, how to do it, or what *not* to do—we will learn about dying from them, and about loving from the way we comfort them at the end.

Death is only the final loss; others come as our mothers approach the end of their lives. Among them is loss of hope when we learn that medical procedures cannot strengthen the frail, cure a fatal illness, or bar the door to death. Then a mother and daughter often draw closer, and a daughter's other responsibilities become secondary while she accompanies her mother through dependence, pain, and fear and—hopefully—into peace. If mothers and daughters still have unresolved emotional conflicts, the final stage can bring perspective, as both let go of what seems superficial in the context of suffering and death. When they are loving friends, this last opportunity for a daughter to serve her mother helps close the circle.

CHAPTER 16

❧

Letting Go When Your Mother Is Your Best Friend

When we think about the relationships between daughters and their aging mothers, it is always in the context of our knowledge that time is short. Virtually every daughter, even those whose mothers have caused them lifelong unhappiness, dreads her mother's death. Whatever else we lose when our mothers die, all of us give up our places as members of a generation once-removed from death.

While conflict and hoped-for resolution play an important part in the last chapter of most mothers and daughters, for daughters who say that their mothers were their best friends—who describe their relationships as companionable, unconflicted, loving, and accepting—facing loss is the dominant chord. They are the daughters of women who had great talents for motherhood; who combined generous hearts, uncritical natures, and lives their daughters could admire; and who recognized their daughters as valuable and separate individuals. The daughters of such mothers are not just willing but truly *want* to do a great deal to repay them, and more: they want to hoard as much time with their mothers as they can, before the time they have together is up.

The women to whom nurturing their mothers comes most naturally are often those who have been close to them all their lives. While the style of their closeness varies from one family to the next and is manifested differently in different ethnic and social milieus, its intensity is the same across the spectrum. The three women whose relationships with their mothers are among the best I heard about grew up in diverse circumstances. Julie, who is sharing the last stage of her mother's life, was brought up in an urban black family with limited financial resources. Karen, whose mother died after a disabling nine-year illness, is descended from Scandinavian homesteaders and was raised in a small town in the Midwest. Melissa, whose mother was bedridden for nearly two years before she died, is the only child of a wealthy Jewish family from Canada. Their stories illustrate that when the time comes to be a good daughter to a mother who is near the end of her life, the daughters of exemplary mothers have much in common. Even women who have had more complicated relationships with their mothers can learn from the way Julie, Karen, and Melissa cared for, and cared about, their mothers in their last years.

When they talk about their mothers, it is not just their particularly unclouded love we hear. They have all been able to take a certain comfort from doing everything possible, and none of them will feel as though a crucial conversation had been interrupted before either person quite managed to make herself clear.

～

JULIE AND ELLA

"She will never really be gone in a spiritual sense."

Julie's mother, Ella, was a role model, both for Julie and for an entire community. Now, in the wake of a series of illnesses, Ella's world is bounded by her small apartment, where her lifelines to the outside world are her children and grandchildren and a phone that still rings all day and well into the night. Julie is preparing herself to let her mother go. It is one of the hardest tasks she has ever faced.

Ella lives on the ground floor in a brownstone garden apartment on an attractive, well-kept street in Harlem. Julie, who lives in her own self-contained apartment on the middle two floors of the house, describes Ella as "telephone central."

"People from the neighborhood call Momma for her help on problems, political leaders call to get her advice," Julie says, "and she's the one who always knows where everyone in the family is."

A couple of years ago, Julie's younger daughter, Eloise, moved to a new school district, and Eloise's son, Jason, changed schools. "Around December, the attendance officer from Jason's old school called Momma to find out where he was," Julie says. "Momma said, 'Why are you calling me?' He told her, 'Because you're the emergency number in his file.' Once she'd gotten that cleared up, Momma gave him hell. 'School started in September and you just now noticed that our little boy is missing?' she asked. 'Is that the way you do your job?' Momma always fought for us while we were growing up, and she's still fighting."

She is. But Ella's biggest fight now is with her body. At seventy-five, only one kidney works, she has high blood pressure and glaucoma, and two years ago she had a stroke that affected the part of the brain whose function Julie describes as "having to do with processing information and being able to give it back out, although it didn't impact her mobility or her coordination. It's hard to tell anything's wrong, but Momma doesn't like to go out because she thinks people recognize that she is not thinking as sharply as she used to. She says to me, 'I don't want to be seen like this.' But when people do see her, they say, 'What is she worrying about? She seems fine.'

"For me, the biggest problem is accepting that she doesn't want to do anything or go anywhere. When the weather is nice, she loves to garden—sometimes she does too much work out there. Otherwise, she stays inside."

It is not hard to understand why Julie is upset that her mother is withdrawing from the world. Ella was once one of the most formidable women in Harlem politics and a leader of the civil rights movement. She was the matriarch of a large family that included her thirteen brothers and sisters and their husbands, wives, and children, as well as her own husband and three children. She was also a handsome woman who was sometimes mistaken for Lena Horne. Julie looks very much like her.

Ella was brought up in North Carolina and moved to New York when she was nineteen. There she worked first as a beautician and then in a clerical position for a federal agency during World War II. That's when she met Julie's father, Leonard, a Pullman porter who was considerably older than she. They married and she quit her clerical job and started a new career as a mother and community activist.

"Momma created a system where both the male district leader and his female coleader, whom he used to appoint, had to be elected, and she was the first elected female district leader in New York City," Julie says. Then Ella worked on the staff of a series of Manhattan Borough presidents. "She was one of the key people to organize Bobby Kennedy's tour of Harlem that got so much attention," Julie says.

Ella was loving and warm at home with her children—Julie has an older sister, who lives in Chicago, and a brother in New York—but she was tough outside in a world that often condescended to both women and blacks. "One of the district leaders she worked with was Italian, and he had a temper. He would get angry at people and punch them out," Julie recalls. "He treated women any way he wanted to, touching them, and he felt he had every right to do that. Momma would say, 'Why do you do this to women?' Then one day they were at a local Democratic club, and he walked by her and patted her on the butt. She opened the window and started throwing things out, and she picked up a chair like she was going to hit him with it. After that, he treated her with a lot more respect."

When her children were little, Ella sometimes took the same approach to protect them. Once a man with a weekend drinking problem who lived in the apartment building where Julie grew up, pushed Julie's ten-year-old sister off the front stoop. "He didn't hurt her badly, but she fell down a couple of stairs. Of course, we ran upstairs crying and told Momma. She got all the information from us: When did this happen? How did it happen? What did he do? The next day I saw her sitting on the stairs with a big butcher knife in her hand. I said, 'What are you doing?' and she said, 'I'm waiting for Mr. Ditmars. I have to talk to him.' When he came home, she followed him into his apartment, and she beat him for hitting her child. The police came, and later she had to go to court. She wasn't very big, maybe five-five, and he was a huge, tall man. She said to the judge, 'How could I beat this man? Look at him and look at me.' She ended up getting a restraining order against him. If he ever heard us coming out in the hallway, he could not come out; he had to wait for us to leave.

"That's how I remember her, but she was also very much a lady, sophisticated and intelligent. She was considered to run for Congress, but she didn't like what she would have to do to get the nomination. I never found out what that was, but she said, 'My integrity is worth more to me.'"

Julie got pregnant when she was in high school. The baby's father was only seventeen, and too immature to marry her, so Julie had her child and then went back to school while Ella and Leonard took care of her daughter. Ella wanted Julie to go away to college and said she would continue to care for the baby, but "that wasn't fair to my parents," Julie says. "So I got a job and went to night school and got my college degree, and then I went on, still at night, and got a graduate degree in social work. At the beginning I lived with my parents, but then I married my daughter's father, so I moved out. It would have been much more difficult without their support and financial aid."

The only serious argument Ella and Julie ever had was

when Julie decided to get married. "Momma just didn't think he was a nice person. At that time, it wasn't as acceptable as it is now to be a single mother. It was still a shame on the family, but Momma would rather have lived with that than to see me unhappy. When I said, 'I'm doing it anyway,' she helped me plan the wedding and hoped it would work out, which it didn't. We had another daughter, but the marriage lasted only a couple of years. That was the biggest conflict between Momma and me. After that, nothing."

In the family circle, although Ella was third youngest of fourteen, she was the leader. "When family members had problems, they came to her with things they needed to resolve, and they waited to see what she was going to say or do. She was the one who organized everything when anyone in the family died," Julie says.

But when Ella was in her sixties and her older siblings began to die at a rate of up to two a year, Ella suddenly backed off.

"I saw the change when one of Momma's sisters died suddenly of a heart attack," Julie says. "Even though my aunt had a husband and daughter, they waited for Momma to come to the house and call the funeral home. But my mother went home and got into bed. I was still at my aunt's house, and I called Momma and said, 'When are we going to start the funeral arrangements?' She said, 'I just can't do anything.' That was the first time I ever saw her quit. I was really shaken. Momma was always able to handle death tremendously well; it's a natural part of life. But now that everyone is dying—a lot of her friends and all but one of her ten sisters—her strength and her ability to deal with difficult situations have changed."

Ella's political life began to slow down about the same

time because Leonard, then in his eighties, developed Alzheimer's disease. "Physically he wasn't that bad, which was part of the problem," Julie says. "He would leave the house and wander around, and sometimes we couldn't find him for twenty-four hours. My mother used to stay up all night to monitor him. He needed more custodial care, and we finally had to put him in a nursing home, but we set up a schedule so that every day someone was there to see him."

Leonard died, and a few years later Ella suffered a stroke. That was when she stopped participating in politics and community affairs. "My biggest issue with my mother's aging is that I think she could do more," Julie says. She has tried to persuade her mother to become involved in community activities again; she suggested that Ella volunteer at a settlement house run by close friends of hers or at a babies' shelter she helped start. "They aren't filled with the negatives of politics, and she could still keep her mind active and continue to give. But she hesitates and says things like, 'I don't want to be committed to have to do anything or be anywhere at any time.' I think she is sicker than she lets on."

Julie says, "I'm trying to respect where Momma is and not impose so much of what I think she should be doing on her, but it's hard." Recently, she remembered that when she was a child, playing on the street, she would see adults come home and go upstairs, and she would think, "'How boring! Don't they want to stay outside and play?' But when I became an adult, I said, 'All right; I understand. I don't want to do that anymore.' You move on to other things. It's still important for me to be active and involved and to socialize. But when I'm seventy, maybe it will be okay for me to be quiet and be at home. So I've given up in that area with Momma. But it does seem like there would be other things she could do that would be pleasurable to her."

The "other things" haven't tempted Ella much, either. Julie gets tickets to a concert or a play she thinks Ella would like, and then she goes downstairs to invite her. "I try to make her feel guilty about not going. I'll say, 'I bought these tickets and they cost thirty-five dollars, so what am I going to do with them now?' I tell her she just has to sit there and listen; she won't have to interact with anybody. Then she agrees to come. But at the last minute, she'll convince my daughter to go instead. So I'm trying to leave her alone about that, too.

"I've asked myself how I can help her best, and although there are some things she won't allow, there are others I can do. I periodically try to get her to the doctor; we found out she had glaucoma because I took her to the eye clinic. Since her stroke, she's had to go to a lot of different doctors. I know it drives her crazy. She never has liked doctors. But we want to know everything is all right. She accepts it, but after a while she gets to a point where she says, 'I'm not going. If I didn't go to the doctor I wouldn't have all these things wrong with me.' I say, 'Yeah, if you didn't go to the doctor you'd probably be dead, and you wouldn't have all these things.' So she'll laugh and say, 'Okay.' She has a good sense of humor."

Julie talks to her mother every day on the phone and sees her most days, too. "If I'm too busy to visit, I'll call and say, 'I'm here, are you okay?' or 'I'm on my way out, do you need anything?'" Julie says. Ella is almost never alone for an entire day. Julie's older daughter has moved into the third floor of the house with her two sons, and when the boys come home from school they often go to

Ella's for help with their homework and a snack; Julie's daughter, who likes to cook and is very close to her grandmother, regularly makes dinner for them all in Ella's apartment.

To enrich Ella's life, Julie shows her that she is still needed. "My father started his downward spiral because he didn't have anything to do. He used to take my children back and forth to school, but when they wanted to go to school by themselves, he felt useless. One of the things Momma does that is really important is to be the information headquarters for all of us. When we are running around and everything is happening, we call her and let her know that we're in such and such a place. She says, 'Don't tell me, because I can't remember and I get mixed up,' but she writes things down and she's still the point of connection. She has also been really helpful in the construction work we're doing on the house. My grandfather and uncles were contractors, so Momma knows how things are supposed to be done. She has played a very critical role in coordinating. She'll check on the workmen, so when I'm at my office, I don't have to worry about what's going on."

Julie has now become the member of her generation the rest of her family turns to for advice. "My sister and I said after the last aunt's funeral, 'We're becoming the senior members of the family. We are the responsible ones.' I thought, 'Oh God, can I do this?' It's a sadness knowing that it's me now, not my mother." Fortunately, when Julie isn't sure what to do, she can call her mother or visit her to talk her problems out. "I share a lot with Momma, and I still look to her, not so much for direction, but for putting things in a proper perspective when they get out of hand. I guess I could say my mother is my best friend."

Ella won't always be there to help Julie keep her life in perspective, and Julie is becoming preoccupied with the prospect of her mother's death. "My brother called me the other day at work because Momma hadn't answered the phone. 'Where is she!' he kept saying. I told him she went to the store. He said, 'Well, she should call me when she leaves the house.' We all know that she could die at any moment, and it's scary."

When Julie finds herself thinking too much about what will happen when her mother dies, she scolds herself. "I am wasting the fact that she is *not* dead and she is here with us. I am thinking, she's going to be dead and maybe she's going to die in her sleep. How is it going to happen, and what am I going to do? And then I say, 'Would you please stop! She's here, and enjoy what you have.'"

When Ella does die, Julie says she will miss her sense of humor, her wisdom, and being able to talk to her. "To put something out there and hear how she's going to respond: I don't think I'll ever be able to replace it. That will be something I have in my memories. But my view of life is that she will never truly be gone in a spiritual sense."

While particular mothers and daughters in all cultures are close, Julie theorizes that the black culture has distinctively strong family ties: "It's very rare that I hear a black daughter saying, 'I don't like my mother; I can't stand being around her.' There's a recognition that you are only here because your mother did the best she could with what she had, and you owe her something.

"We have a long history of being connected to our mothers. My grandmother in Virginia at some time raised all her grandchildren, except us. It wasn't a matter of single parenthood or economic necessity; many of the parents were married and had good jobs. It was what you were supposed to do. Your mother's there to help you raise your children and, as a child, you're supposed to be with your grandmother sometimes. Then, when we're grown, we're supposed to help our mothers. It's always a back and forth; you are so connected there's no time when you are ever supposed to cut it off. Whatever is going on in your family is not as important as that you *have* a family. That means we are supposed to be helpful and supportive of each other. It doesn't mean that we are always going to agree.

"This is an obligation, but it's not a burden. It's part of the natural flow, and without that, I would be uncomfortable."

Julie's instinct about the ties among black families is confirmed by a study recently conducted for the National Institute on Aging by Raymond T. Coward, dean of health and human services at the University of New Hampshire. He found that "older blacks are twice as likely as whites to receive care from family members when their health declines." More than one-third of black people over sixty-five live in multigenerational homes—nearly double the 18 percent of whites of the same age who live with younger family members. One woman who has cared for both her mother-in-law and her mother explained, "It all goes back to slavery. Family was all anyone had."[1]

The thread of spirituality, Julie says, is another strong element in African-American culture. "It has always been a part of who we were. One aspect of spirituality is homage to your ancestors: they are always with you, and they continue to play a major role in your life."

Julie has learned a lot, not just from her culture but

from her own quite exceptional mother. Julie's respect for Ella is so solid that she is not tempted to condescend to her; instead, she has tried to imagine Ella's perspective and empathize with her need to wind down. Julie may mourn the powerhouse of a mother she once had, but she is sensitive enough to recognize that Ella has had to leave that behind. By trying to understand her mother's point of view—remembering that, as a child, she couldn't understand why adults wouldn't want to play outside when they came home from work—Julie has acknowledged that what is appropriate at one stage may no longer make sense in the next.

Rather than making the sweeping judgment that, just because she can do so much less than she once did, Ella can't do *anything*, Julie has found realistic ways for Ella to be a useful member of the family. That helps Ella retain her self-respect, gives her something interesting to do, and because her role really *is* useful, she contributes to everyone's lives.

When a daughter replaces her mother as the functional head of the family, she needs to be careful not to become a bully or rob her mother of her autonomy. Julie has been sparing about the way she uses her power; she doesn't push her mother too hard, except when it is really important. She tries to encourage her mother to go out, but she backs off and doesn't make Ella feel guilty when she refuses. When Ella needs to go to a doctor, however, Julie is insistent.

As it becomes clear that a mother's life will end soon, many daughters want to spend more time with their mothers. Even if Ella lives for five more years and during that time the balance of Julie's life is tipped toward her, perhaps at the cost of a more active social life, Julie says she will always be glad she has adapted her priorities. One thing Julie won't do: she can't afford to stop working to care for her mother, even if she wanted to give up or suspend her career. Ella wouldn't want her to do that, either, and she has made it clear that if she can't care for herself, she expects her children to move her into a nursing home. Ella knows that her family will not just drop her off and only make "duty calls" but will set up a schedule so one of them visits her every day.

Finally, Julie's admonition to herself not to start grieving for her mother while she is still alive is a helpful reminder to other daughters who worry about the future at the cost of getting the most out of the present. Her attitude is reminiscent of Robert Butler's observation that the elderly, who can't look ahead to many years of life, learn to live each day as it comes.

~

KAREN AND TINA

"You can do everything for your mother, but when she dies, you still feel terrible."

Some people get sick, seem to be on the brink of death, and then, even in their eighties, recover to lead relatively healthy lives. Others are disabled by illness, and it is evident to them, their families, and their doctors that they are facing irreversible disintegration and death. People of any age often say, "I hope I die in my sleep" or "I just hope when it's my turn, it's quick and painless." But often it is *slow* and *painful,* and a good daughter may have to put aside other interests and obligations for a time because her mother needs her.

It may be peculiarly American to look for opportunities in even the least promising situations—and it doesn't seem to be an unreasonable hope. Uncovering "opportunities" in a fatal illness challenges even the most optimistic, but they exist, particularly in opening a kind of intimacy that is an intrinsic part of taking care of someone who is helpless and sometimes frightened.

Karen chose to be the principal caretaker to her mother when she became severely disabled, and her caretaking continued with increasing intensity for nine years. How did she feel about spending nearly a decade on call night and day? She wouldn't have had it any other way.

Karen is so devastated by the death of her mother, Tina, that she can't stop herself from crying whenever (and wherever) she thinks about her. She and her friend Diana, whose mother died shortly after Tina did, talk on the phone all the time and meet in coffee shops to commiserate. "We sit there and we look so gloomy—and then we laugh that anyone we know who sees us will think we're having marital problems," Karen says. It has been only four months since Tina died, and Karen hopes that her sorrow will become less sharp as time passes. "But then I'm afraid that my memories of my mother will lose their edge, too," she says.

Tina, the child of homesteaders in the Dakotas, moved to a small town in Minnesota after she was married, and there she brought up her daughters, Karen and Linda. Her husband ran a general store and farm equipment leasing business; Tina managed his office. Tina's mother, whom everyone called Grammy, lived with them until she died, at ninety-three. Tina played the piano and sang, so their small suburban ranch house was filled with music. Grammy baked every day, so it always smelled of cookies and cakes. Breakfasts were likely to be pancakes Grammy made in animal shapes. There was never any trouble getting the children to bed because Tina would go in with them, lie down on one of the girls' beds, and play phonics games with them ("I'm thinking of something in this room that starts with a *C* "), or Grammy would come in and tell them stories about her childhood in a sod house on the prairie. Karen ran home from school every day to be with her mother and grandmother.

Home was so happy that Karen had a hard time settling down when she went away to college. For a while, her homesickness was severe enough that her parents arranged for her to live with her sorority "mother"; later, she dropped out of college a couple of times and went home, then returned, and managed to graduate in four years.

Karen and her sister, Linda, moved to Los Angeles after college, and Karen began a career in investment banking. A couple of years later, Karen's father and grandmother died within six weeks of each other, and Tina, now a widow, moved to California to be near her daughters. Karen, who is attractive and easy company, had plenty of dates, but she hadn't found anyone she wanted to marry. Often she took vacations with her mother, and they shared a room. Karen and Linda and her family spent summer vacations at Tina's cottage on a lake in Minnesota.

In her thirties, Karen left California, got a good job on Wall Street, and attended law school at night. When she was studying for her bar exams, Tina moved in with her in New York for most of the summer and cooked for her so Karen could study without interruption and then go to her evening cram course. Karen, well loved, well fed, and well prepared, passed on the first try. "My mother was totally unjudgmental, but she set the highest standards for my sister and me, and we always knew she was cheering us on, rather than driving us," Karen says.

The year Karen turned forty, she started a nonprofit law practice and married a partner in one of the top Wall Street investment banking firms. She had been married for two years when Tina, who was in her early seventies, had a stroke. Karen, who still spoke to her mother every day, was the first person to figure out that something was wrong. "I was on the phone with Mama, who was in Minnesota. We were talking, and I mentioned an old friend of hers. She said, 'I don't know who that is.' I got off the phone fast and called a neighbor to go over there. An hour later, Mama was in an ambulance, on her way to the hospital."

Tina was both mentally and physically disabled by the stroke. (She never learned to read again, although she did regain her speech and her ability to walk.) It was then that Karen had the opportunity to repay her mother. She arranged for Tina to move to New York and found an apartment for her a couple of blocks from Karen and her husband. Karen hired and oversaw an aide, but she did much of the caretaking herself. She planned each day for her mother. She took her to the movies, the theater, concerts, museum lectures, lunch, and shopping. She spoke to her every day, as she always had. She stopped by Tina's apartment when Tina was home in bed and lay on the second bed in her room, and the two of them chatted for hours, like roommates. For Tina's eightieth birthday,

Karen and Linda and their husbands took her on a trip to the one place she wanted to go: Las Vegas.

For nine years, Tina was at the center of Karen's world, but she wasn't the only centerpiece. Karen's marriage was successful, and so was her legal aid practice, which started with a single lawyer (Karen) and grew to seventy-five lawyers.

In the last few years of Tina's life, she was increasingly besieged by many of the problems that can beset people as they become old and sick: she was nearly blind, she had intermittent dementia, and, finally, she was confined to a wheelchair.

The daily pressures of Tina's condition became overwhelming toward the end. Tina had Karen's phone on automatic dial, and there were times when she called her twenty times in an hour. She had bursts of defiant independence when she would wait for the aide to go on an errand and then sneak out of her apartment. Karen would get a call from Tina's vigilant doorman. "Your mother's gone exploring again. She's headed toward Madison Avenue," he would report. Then Karen would run out and look for Tina. On one of those expeditions, Tina fell in a pothole and knocked out her front teeth; on another, she wandered into an optometrist's shop, thinking it was her doctor's office. Karen took Tina to church, and Tina thought she saw her mother, who had been dead for decades, and kept calling out to her. Tina's aide took her to the park, and Tina, walking alongside her wheelchair, suddenly got frightened that Karen was lost and began to run after a little girl, then tripped, fell, and had to be taken to the emergency room.

Yet Tina continued to have bursts of clarity when her sense of humor and reality would appear in their full colors. Karen waited for them and savored the times when Tina's personality broke through. Even a few days before she died, when Tina, weighing eighty pounds and disoriented, was in the hospital with pneumonia, she had moments when she was very much herself. The last conversation she had with her older grandson, a couple of days before she died, went like this:

"How're you doing, Grandma?"

"Fine. Start the car," Tina said.

"Where are we going?"

"Anywhere," Tina declared and gave him a conspiratorial grin.

"I wanted my mother to have the best life possible," Karen says. "For each day to be the best it could be for her. A lot of people feel there is something they should have said to their mothers or done for them, but there was nothing left unsaid between us. We never talked about death; Mama was more interested in life. I had my arms around her every day, and she was never alone. If my mother were alive, I'd rather be with her than anyone else except my husband. But the last year was tough, and I don't know how much longer I could have done it. It got so I couldn't take a deep breath without shaking.

"You can do everything for your mother, and you can know that her life had become very difficult, but, when she dies, you still feel terrible. I can never replace her. The best thing I can do for her is to heal myself. A mother's gift to her children is to teach them to fly. That's what Mama would want me to do and I'm trying, but it's still very hard."

Other daughters whose mothers need a great deal of care and attention do as much as Karen did—Grace was another particularly dutiful daughter to her mother, Mary Rose—but Karen's problems in Tina's old age did not involve guilt, ambivalence, or resentment. For her, the worst part of her mother's decline was that she worried about her safety and happiness, and she was afraid that she would die. One explanation for Karen's ability to care for her mother, start a substantial organization, and begin a new marriage is that she really *wanted* to do all three. If taking care of Tina had felt like a burden to her, it would have used up emotional energy she needed for the other parts of her life.

Karen's ability to pay for the aide her mother required gave her a certain freedom. But Julie, who works full-time, is single, and just manages to support herself and pay the mortgage on the house she shares with her mother, is as attentive as Karen. The difference between their financial situations will become more apparent if Ella needs full-time care, which Julie can't afford. Then Ella will have to move to a nursing home, but Julie will still be on call—willingly—every day.

~

MELISSA AND VICTORIA

"I have no regrets."

Competition isn't inevitable in a mother-daughter relationship, even when appearance is important to both of them. And distance doesn't always attenuate their bonds; in some cases, living in different cities can enable a daughter to develop her own identity and way of life without causing conflicts that might arise if they lived a few blocks apart.

Melissa, an only child, had an exceptionally close relationship with her mother, the dauntingly elegant and confident Victoria. Their love and respect for each other was so firmly established that Melissa wasn't thrown off by issues about appearance that would have pushed the hot buttons of most daughters. Their roles remained clear until the end of Victoria's life. Even when Victoria was bedridden, her attitude toward her daughter reflected more maternal concern than dependence.

During Victoria's final illness, Melissa chose to disrupt her life to be a good daughter. Fortunately, she could afford to fly from New York to Toronto, where her mother lived, every week for nearly two years, and her financial security distinguishes her from many daughters. Yet the essence of her relationship with her mother and the way it led to a deeply satisfying end for both of them, provide a model that reflects considerably more about love and respect than it does about class or money.

Melissa smiles when she picks up a silver-framed photograph taken when Victoria was in her seventies. "Only my mother could wear a hat like that," Melissa says.

The hat in question is enormous and black, its huge brim trimmed with white feathers that seem to be fluttering in a little breeze. The face under the hat is strong enough to hold its own, even under that extravagant millinery creation. The eyes are intelligent and lively, the cheekbones high, and the nose beaked. The rest of the outfit is smart: a boldly patterned black-and-white silk dress and matching coat hang perfectly on a slim, straight-backed frame; chorus-girl legs and narrow feet in high-heeled shoes complete the picture. "Mother often looked as though she was on her way to see the queen," Melissa says, "or maybe I should say she looked like a queen herself."

Melissa is exceptionally attractive too, although she doesn't look like her mother: Melissa is softer, blond, with delicate features and fair skin. She, too, is stylish, but her style is more casual and less dramatic. Her everyday uniform is liable to be a cream-colored cashmere sweater with a double strand of pearls, a gray flannel skirt, and neat, well-polished pumps.

Melissa grew up in a formal, old-fashioned household, supported by the wealth created by her maternal grandfather's department store and her father's successful law practice. Her family's dedication to community service leavened the sense of luxury. Melissa's grandparents and parents were well known for their charitable activities. In the late 1930s and early 1940s, Melissa's grandmother brought boatloads of Jewish refugees from Europe to Canada after they were refused entry to the United States. For that and other wartime activities, she was awarded the OBE (Order of the British Empire), the first woman and the first Jewish Canadian to receive that honor.

"Granny was an amazing woman and my mother worshiped her," Melissa says, "but Granny was so busy that her children didn't know her very well. My mother didn't want to have that kind of relationship with me. Mother had breakfast with me every day, and she was always home at four o'clock when I got back from school. She was involved in all kinds of civic and cultural causes—she started the national ballet company, and I remember when she went to England to interview ballet mistresses—but she was a mother first."

Although Victoria was a regular on the best-dressed list in Canada, Melissa says, "Mother cared about her appearance, but she didn't care about lists. She may have looked grand, but she had good values and she was well rooted. She made sure I understood what was really important and had a sense of proportion about money. We'd go shopping and, if I looked at a dress that was too expensive, Mother would say, 'That dress is not for you; the price tag is a telephone number.' I remember once, when a saleslady tried to talk us into buying something that was ridiculously extravagant, Mother asked her if she thought a little girl should wear a dress that cost enough to feed a family for a week." Victoria was particularly vigilant that her daughter was aware of how fortunate she was. "Mother used to say, 'Never look at those who have more; look at those who have less, and thank your lucky stars every day,' " Melissa says.

Victoria was strict—"She acted like a mother when I was growing up; she didn't try to be my friend," Melissa explains—yet she wasn't distant. "Mother was always interested in me and my friends. She listened to them when their own mothers didn't. After Mother died, I got wonderful letters from women I'd grown up with, reminding me of how everyone always wanted to go home with me after school because my mother was such fun to be with.

"Mother taught me to stand tall," Melissa says. "I was the only Jewish girl in my class at school. When I came home from school and told her that my teacher said the Jews killed Christ, Mother called the headmistress. The next day the teacher recanted in front of the class. I knew that, whatever happened, I could tell my mother and she would believe me and back me up."

Melissa got through her adolescence without butting heads with her mother very often. "Whatever she said, I agreed to," she says. "I adored Mother, she never put me down, and she was usually right." But when Melissa graduated from college, she and Victoria had a major argument. Melissa wanted to move out of her parents' house and live on her own, but Victoria refused to consider it. "Mother was out of her mind about the very idea," Melissa says, but before their disagreement escalated, the point became moot. Melissa fell in love with an American doctor, and they became engaged and were married. Finally, Melissa left home to move to New York City, where her new husband had an appointment at a teaching hospital.

After Melissa was married, she and her mother began to make the transition to a more equal friendship. Although distance gave Melissa a chance to develop her own life, she and her mother stayed in constant contact. "People used to ask me if I talked to my mother every day, and I would say, 'Ask me how many times a day.' It had to be hard for her to have me so far away," Melissa says, "but she never said, 'I'm lonesome for you.'"

Melissa was beginning to find that she and her mother didn't always agree. "Our basic values were the same, but our style was different," she says. "Mother knew nothing about the kitchen; she had never cooked. When I'd say, 'What'll I do about dinner?' she would say, 'Change your clothes before your husband comes home, then give him a martini, and the rest will take care of itself.' But we didn't live the way she and Dad did. We couldn't afford to have that kind of a household, and we wouldn't have wanted to if we could have."

Melissa had two children, a daughter and a son, and she did listen to her mother's advice about raising them. "When the kids had problems, she always had good, practical opinions about what to do," she says. But in the 1970s, Melissa and Victoria had another disagreement. "The children were in school, a lot of my friends were going back to work, and I wanted to get a job," Melissa says. "My husband was supportive, but Mother said, 'You belong at home.' If I had stayed in Canada, I would have done what Mother told me to do—I would have been her daughter, rather than my own person." But with her mother's influence attenuated by distance, Melissa had more breathing room, and she found a job at a public relations company.

"Mother thought my marriage would fall apart and the children would be a mess. She announced that she was coming to New York to talk to me about it. I said I was too busy to see her, but she said, 'You take lunch, don't you?'

"When we went out to lunch, she said, 'I hope you're enjoying this job, because you look terrible.' I *was* exhausted, but I was making a point to myself, that I could work, still be a good, full-time mother, and keep giving 'perfect' dinner parties. I didn't really *love* the job, although I liked it enough, but after a couple of years, I became convinced that Mother was right: it wasn't doing the family any good. I began to think about stopping after my husband took the children on a vacation without me because my boss told me the office was too busy for me to take the time off I was due. Then one day, I got a call from my son to say the police were at the house because someone had stolen his skateboard. I thought, okay, this is not my dream career, my husband can support the family without my help, I could be a lot more useful as a volunteer, and it wouldn't disrupt my family. Since then, I've been what I'd call a 'professional volunteer.'"

Meanwhile, Melissa's parents were both healthy and active. When her father retired, they bought a winter house in Mexico, which became the center for family vacations. Just as Melissa's friends had loved Victoria, Victoria's grandchildren adored her, too. Victoria, who was notably unathletic, would play baseball with her grandchildren, and their lively family dinners included the children as soon as they were old enough. On New Year's Eve, everyone dressed up, and the children put on magic shows or skits.

Victoria provided emotional support as well as entertainment. If one of Melissa's children was sick, sometimes Victoria would get on a plane and come down to help. One winter when Victoria was in Mexico, Melissa's husband contracted a rare virus and was in the hospital. Melissa asked her housekeeper not to tell her mother how sick he was when she called, but the housekeeper was too upset to keep the secret and burst into tears on the phone. The next day, Melissa was sitting by her husband's hospital bed when Victoria arrived. "'I'll handle everything at home,' Mother said. 'Don't think about anything except your husband. And when you're thinking about him, don't let in a single negative thought.'"

So when Melissa's father had his first heart attack, *she* took the first plane to Canada to support her mother. "I'd just had my hair colored and it was too blond," Melissa says. "When I walked into Daddy's hospital room, my mother said, 'You look like a flashlight!' Maybe another daughter would have been annoyed, but I didn't resent it. Mother was right, and she was the one person who would tell me. Mother didn't resent it, either, when *she* came to see *me* and I said, 'Mother, your hair's like patent leather.' We just went to my hairdresser and got it lightened."

Over the next ten years, Melissa's father had a series of heart attacks, although, in between, he continued to be active and alert. The week before he died, at ninety-five, Melissa says, "He beat me at gin rummy."

Victoria's reaction to her husband's death was to maintain her composure, even with her daughter. "I did catch her crying in her bedroom one afternoon," Melissa says. "But she said, 'Don't pay any attention to me; I'm just a little tired.' There were some things Mother didn't talk about. Death was one of them. Sex was another. That's the way women of her generation were."

Two years after her husband died, Victoria developed congestive heart failure. She tried to keep the news from Melissa, who was traveling in the Far East with her husband. "I called her regularly, even when I was on a trip. Her housekeeper answered the phone and told me, 'Your mother is not well,' but Mother convinced me it wasn't serious. As soon as I got back, I went to see her, and she was bedridden. It was like being a cardiac cripple."

With Victoria unable to leave the house, Melissa established the arduous schedule that she kept up for the last two years of her mother's life. Every Sunday night, she flew to Canada and stayed until Tuesday, then returned in time to have dinner with her husband. "Mother always made sure I went back home on Tuesday, even when she didn't feel well. She would say, 'This is so awful for you, dear,' and she would pat my face. She was so sweet.

"The nurses adored her, and she was interested in

them the way she had always been interested in other people. One day, one of the nurses came in, and Mother said, 'Something's bothering you. Sit down and tell me what's on your mind.' The nurse's daughter had a learning problem, and Mother got on the phone and helped her find a special program. As long as I can remember, she helped others. I don't know how many college educations she paid for."

The first year Victoria was ill, she and Melissa often talked about the past. "We both loved to remember the things we did when I was growing up, the trips she and Daddy took with me. Or I would tell her about my life, board meetings, the children's news, my husband's practice. Mother was a great listener, and she always made me feel that I was valuable to her as a person. I knew that she loved and liked me, even if she didn't like everything I did. We talked about almost everything—but Mother still didn't want to talk about death."

By the second year of her illness, Victoria's mental faculties were beginning to fray. Her memory was poor, she couldn't think of words, and often she lost track of what she was saying. Sometimes she would indicate that she understood that "she was losing it," as Melissa says. "She would say, 'Maybe I'm having a bad day' or 'I'm forgetful. Did I tell you this already?'" Even when Victoria wasn't sharp, though, Melissa says, "I felt better talking to her."

Finally, Victoria got out of bed and fell and broke her hip. It was a fatal accident. Within a few days, she had begun to drift in and out of a coma. Melissa flew up to stay with her at home—Victoria had always said she didn't want to die in a hospital—and this time Melissa didn't leave. The doctors said Victoria was near death, yet she kept hanging on. "I know she was worried about me,"

Melissa says. "I don't think she wanted me to be alone when she died. Then my daughter called and said she was coming to stay with me. I went in and told Mother, although I didn't think she could hear me. But she opened her eyes and said, 'That's lovely.'"

Victoria died shortly after her granddaughter arrived. "We were sitting on either side of her, both holding her hands," Melissa says. "I was so lucky to have my daughter with me. But even though it was horrible for Mother to be bedridden, and it was her time and she knew it, I was still unprepared to let her go."

After Victoria's funeral, Melissa stayed home and grieved privately, following her mother's example. "I didn't go out for six weeks," Melissa says. "I didn't want to inflict my tears on other people. But it's been a couple of months now, and I'm starting to live my life again.

"When you lose your last parent, you face your own mortality. I'm not ready for that; I have too much living to do. Seeing my mother die has made me appreciate each day of my life more. I used to get concerned about minutiae, but this has given me a better sense of perspective about what's important. I want to enjoy it all, to take everything in and ask for more.

"I hate to think of facing life without Mother, but I know that I can always talk to her in my mind, even if I will hear the answer in my voice, rather than hers. If I could tell other women one thing I've learned from the last two years, it is that I am so pleased now that I did everything I did for her. I have no regrets."

It's interesting that appearance, which was important to both Victoria and Melissa, was such a neutral feature on their emotional landscape. Victoria never turned appearance into a competitive sport with her daughter. Both she and Melissa were confident enough about the way they looked that they could even critique each other without creating bad feelings. And because the subject of looks wasn't highly charged, Melissa could laugh and agree when Victoria said that her hair was as bright as a flashlight—a comment few daughters could take with good grace.

Victoria always treated Melissa with respect, and she both expected and earned Melissa's respect in return. A curious element of their relationship is that, although they were so close, they seem to have had a clear sense of appropriate boundaries. Even when they had real disagreements, such as over whether Melissa should work, Melissa knew that making an adult decision her mother didn't approve of would not damage their relationship. And when Melissa decided she would rather spend more time with her family than work at a salaried job, she could admit that her mother was right without worrying about saving face or expecting her mother to use the experience to demonstrate that she knew best the next time they disagreed.

Some mothers and daughters are lucky: they are innately well matched. Those who don't fit together quite as well may have more difficulty, but Victoria and Melissa's example at least shows others how well a mother and daughter get along when they don't let small comments or more substantive differences of opinion interfere with their relationship.

How can daughters whose history with their mothers is *not* as consistently amicable as Victoria and Melissa's defuse old issues late in life? Perhaps the sense of perspective Melissa spoke of when she looked back on her mother's last years can blur the irritation. "Time is short; hair doesn't matter" wouldn't be a bad mantra, especially if a daughter hopes to be able to say, as Melissa did, "I have no regrets."

CHAPTER 17

⌒

Making Peace with an Imperfect Mother

ALISON AND BEATRICE

"I wished it would be over, and then I wished it wouldn't be over."

What of the daughter whose mother has not been as easy to love as Ella, Tina, and Victoria? Daughters who have more complicated relationships with their mothers are also faced with intense responsibility and intimate interaction when their mothers become mortally ill. When death is clearly imminent, many such women find that the issues that attend dying put other feelings—even the need for approval, a history of competition, and disappointments—in perspective. Time is short, and a daughter's attention is focused on helping her mother make decisions about health care and pain management, as well as last-minute legacies and funeral plans. Most of all, a daughter wants to comfort her mother—and herself.

The majority of Americans die in hospitals, where treatment is the traditional priority, and death, even of the very old, has overtones of failure. Yet the end of life provides a chance for growth and a uniquely intense intimacy.

It helps if a daughter understands what is happening. The seminal study,[1] Elisabeth Kübler-Ross's *On Death and Dying* (first published in 1969 and still in print), demarcates the stages most people who are dying pass through. Beginning with "awareness of fatal illness," the trajectory is shock, denial, anger, depression, bargaining, acceptance (which overlaps with preparatory grief), and letting go. The attitudes of each phase sometimes blend and recur, and hope is a theme until the last. Kübler-Ross's stages of dying are a useful map of feelings a daughter may observe in her mother as she makes the transitions from one phase to the next.

When someone is in her final illness, certain concerns become paramount. First is that she suffer as little pain as possible and that she is cared for in a way that enables her to preserve her dignity and her connection to those she loves. If she is beyond medical intervention, the emphasis changes from the medical to the personal, and the goal becomes to enhance the quality of the time that is left. Women who have cared for their dying mothers, whether in the hospital or at home, often say that their mothers responded with pleasure to a favorite pillow or blanket, flowers, photographs, quiet music, and letters and cards. Often daughters speak of washing or brushing their mothers' hair, giving backrubs, and feeding them. This caretaking can be difficult for some because of cultural restraints against physical intimacy and because of the repugnance that signs of illness evokes, yet for most people touch is an important source of comfort.

The other common characteristic of the end of life is a heightened urgency to sum up what one has done and what it added up to. In her book, *Intimate Death*, Marie de Hennezel, whose hospice unit in Paris is a model of care for the dying—so much so that, when French president François Mitterrand was diagnosed with fatal cancer, he asked de Hennezel to consult with him—has written that she has often observed among her patients a desire "to tell the story of one's life before one dies." She explains, "There is a need to give shape to one's life and to show this shape, which gives it its meaning, to someone else. Once the telling of it has been accomplished, the person seems to be able to let go, and to die."[2] A daughter can help by listening or by telling her mother's story to her, pointing out her successes and reassuring her that she understands and forgives her failures.

The need to "do something," to talk and to listen, can be frustrated when a mother begins to drift into a semiconscious or comatose state. De Hennezel writes reassuringly of this stage of waiting and watching: "I have learned to keep silent vigil with those who are asleep, or in a coma, and I have discovered the pleasure of just being there . . . being a presence, alert, attentive." The simple sharing of someone else's suffering means being with him or her, not leaving that person alone."[3] De Hennezel continues, "When one's intimacy is rooted in another person's and one feels a deep rapport, silence can feel like a benediction."[4] She adds, "The words it is still possible to exchange, shared glances, the feeling of skin on skin, become irreplaceable."[5]

As each day takes a mother closer to the end, her daughter's emotions are increasingly intense and focused. This level of engagement is too powerful to sustain over a long period; it is possible because there is so little time left, and every moment is important. The strong feelings of love and grief that come at the end emotionally drain the survivor, but they can also be deeply gratifying because they allow her to experience unrestrained and open love.

This can be particularly valuable for mothers and daughters who have had difficult relationships. That was true of Alison, whose mother, Beatrice, was self-absorbed and competitive with her daughter. But when Beatrice was diagnosed with a widely metastasized cancer, Alison was quickly plunged into a concentrated period during which she and her eighty-seven-year-old father, Peter, were Beatrice's most constant emotional support. Alison found that, while this last phase of her mother's life didn't solve all their problems, it put them in perspective.

Alison and Beatrice lived in the same city and had friends and many interests in common, especially in the performing arts. But their values often clashed, and Beatrice was unwilling to admit that hers was not the only—or even the best—way for Alison to lead her life. Alison still feels some of the bitterness that attended their disagreements. "Mother wanted to give me a party for my tenth anniversary, even though I begged her not to. I told her my marriage was collapsing and it seemed hypocritical to celebrate. So she gave me a surprise party instead. I was furious: it was a complete sham; my husband and I were separated within three months of our anniversary. Then, when I turned forty a couple of years later, Mother wanted to give me a party again. I said, 'No. I just want to have a small family dinner.' She did the same thing, planned a party against my wishes and invited a lot of people. That time I found out and refused to go. I told her it was my birthday—my life—and I wasn't going to let her bully me. Mother didn't cancel the party; she just told everyone I couldn't come because I had the flu. Those parties were symbols of the way she refused to understand me. She cared about the way things looked; I care more about the way they *are*."

Only a few months before Beatrice got sick, Alison was invited to join the board of an experimental theater company. When she called to tell her mother, Beatrice's response had been dismissive. "I've heard they're really struggling," she said. "Are you sure you want to get involved with a company that might fail?" Alison explains, "Mother only wanted to be part of something that was already prestigious. But I like to get involved with projects that really need help. Mother certainly deflated my excitement."

But when Beatrice was diagnosed with terminal cancer, interchanges like the one about the theater board were the last thing on Alison's mind. First, she and her parents had to decide whether to accept the doctor's recommendation of medical intervention, even though he had conceded that the treatment would make Beatrice feel wretched and probably extend her life by only a short time.

"My father wanted to do anything possible," Alison says. "My mother thought about it and decided to do nothing. Nobody mentioned the word *death* or talked about how long Mother might live, but she must have understood that the disease was fatal. To see if she wanted to talk about it, I asked her, 'How do you feel about all this?' She said, 'I'm not afraid for myself. I just feel bad because it will be hard for you.' Then she told me the oddest thing. A man who was the chairman of a big multinational company had recently died, and Mother had saved his obituary. 'He accomplished so much,' she said. 'I'm disappointed in myself because I didn't do enough with my life.' I guess that's the sort of summing up people do at the end. I wanted to reassure her that you don't have to be a corporate chairman for your life to matter, but I couldn't think how to do it without sounding as though I was just trying to cheer her up."

One afternoon, sitting by her mother's bed, Alison said, "Remember the obituary you showed me? It started me thinking of all the things you have done. It's quite a list."

"Yes, darling?" Beatrice said, and sat up a bit in bed.

Alison smiles, remembering. "So we talked about the things Mother was proud of, and although neither of us acknowledged what we were doing, in effect, we wrote her obituary together.

"It was a pretty impressive list. She was an artist, she had been a member of the OSS in World War II on the ground in France, and a week after her illness was diagnosed, she was still going to board meetings of the charities she worked so hard for."

Beatrice didn't attend the meetings for much longer. Within a month of the time her cancer was identified, she was bedridden. She left her house for the last time to go to Christmas dinner at Alison's. "Mother couldn't even hold a spoon by then, and one of the memories I will have with me all my life is watching my son feed his grandmother so gently and lovingly, teasing her a little, getting her to take just another taste," Alison says.

Beatrice and Peter made the decision that Beatrice would stay at home until the end, rather than going to a hospital. They had long-term insurance that covered nursing care, but Alison arrived at their apartment every morning after breakfast, often had lunch with her father, spent the early afternoon with her mother, then went back to her own apartment to return phone calls—many of which were from her friends or from friends of her mother's who were calling for news. In the evenings, Alison went back to have dinner with her father. Sometimes Alison's grown children fielded phone calls, and one of them visited their grandmother every day, so when Beatrice became too weak to talk, she could listen to the conversation between Alison and a grandchild.

The nurses on duty were "wonderful," Alison says, and her mother liked them. "But there was still a lot for me to do. Whenever Mother was awake, she had to take her medications and be fed, and sometimes she had coughing fits, and we had to get her to expectorate. She was always very particular about the way she looked, so I brushed her hair and put a little makeup on her and changed her night-gown, or I helped her use the commode. Those weren't the sort of things I would have expected to be comfortable doing, but it seemed natural."

Marie de Hennezel describes accompanying the dying as "an unforgettable opportunity to experience true inti-macy,"[6] and that is the way Alison began to feel. "When my children were babies, I used to watch them for hours, entranced by each little change of expression, every smile or tiny response. I felt that way about my mother at the end," she says. "She didn't talk much, but I tried to get her to react a little, even if it was only a smile or a nod. She knew what was going on around her until the last week or so; she could still follow a conversation, especially when her grandchildren were around. One afternoon, we were standing around her bed, chatting, and I was stroking her hair, and she fell asleep with the loveliest smile on her face. I felt very close to her then."

Among the best experiences for both Alison and Beatrice during those last months was the warmth Alison's three children showed for their mother and grandmother. "My children are in their twenties," Alison says. "They're just starting out on their own and working hard. I didn't want to lean on them, but they were always there for their grandmother and for me. They gave up a lot while my mother was sick, to visit her and stay for dinner with their grandfather. And they helped me keep my perspective so I could look forward rather than just back.

"When your mother dies, you do some life review of your own. One of the things I've looked at is the way I've raised my children. I was very proud of the way they rallied. We learned a lot about the strength of our family to pull together. One of the things we're doing when we go through something like this is preparing the next generation to face losing us."

Alison noticed that the anger with her mother that had simmered below the surface of their relationship for so long began to dissipate. "That all felt petty," she says. "The things that were unresolved were my problems, not hers. I had a certain perception of the relationship I would have liked to have had with my mother, but I tried to let go of that. My biggest conflict was with myself: I wished it would be over, and then I wished it wouldn't be over."

It is not unusual for family members to displace on each other their feelings about the person who is dying, rather than exposing someone who is ill to too much emotion. Alison found that both she and her father sometimes vented their anger, frustration, and grief by snapping at each other. Alison was particularly upset because her father was unable to come to terms with the reality that Beatrice was dying. His denial clouded his judgment, while his grief ignited his temper.

"Dad was ten years older than Mother. Although they had talked about what would happen if one of them got sick and they agreed neither of them wanted any desperate measures to be taken to prolong their lives, I'm sure Dad thought Mother would be the one to make the decisions. He has a heart condition, and he probably expected that he would have a fast crisis, like a heart attack; instead, he was faced with her protracted death. The scripts we imagine aren't always the ones we're handed," Alison says.

"When the pain became really bad, the doctor told my father that heavy doses of morphine would shorten Mother's life and suggested they cut down. That didn't seem very smart to me, but my father said, 'I'm not killing Beatrice,' and told the doctor to try giving her less morphine. My mother would have to be in agony to complain, but I could see from the expression on her face that she wasn't getting enough painkiller. I confronted my father and told him that he was being cruel, and he finally agreed that the morphine could be increased again."

Beatrice had been sick for three months when she died. It was just after dawn on an early winter day, and Peter was there with her, although Alison, who had hoped to hold her mother's hand at the end, was at home, asleep. Alison made sure that Beatrice's obituary notice in the paper was long and filled with her accomplishments, Alison and her father organized a stately and elegant funeral that reflected Beatrice's sense of style, and Alison's children spoke with grace and presence about their grandmother. At the end of the funeral service, Peter took the rose out of his buttonhole, kissed it, and placed it on Beatrice's casket. Then, straightening his shoulders, gripping his cane, and marching behind the casket with his children and grandchildren, Peter made his way down the aisle of the church. Alison, straight-backed and chic in a large black hat, held his arm while he stopped at every pew to shake hands and accept condolences, while the tears streaked his cheeks.

It seemed complete, that afternoon in the church, as though the ends were neatly tied up. And yet . . . "I know that my mother couldn't undo our whole history before she died," Alison says, "but I can't help wishing our relationship had been different. Mother thought it was better than I did. Perhaps it's a generational idea: to 'relate' may be more formal and less intimate for my mother's generation, and maybe I expected too much. Even at the end, I was disappointed that Mother didn't understand me, my ambitions about my work, and my lack of the kind of social ambitions that were important to her.

"I keep on telling myself that you love each other the best you can and you do the best you can, but, if I am honest with myself, I have to admit it isn't really enough."

This may be the last and hardest lesson, and I have spoken of it before. Life is untidy; relationships are unruly; we are imperfect. In our eagerness to connect, succeed, and be acknowledged by our mothers, we can ask too much of ourselves and of them.

We are anxious to force conclusions, but in this it seems that we will be thwarted and must wait. My own father has been dead for ten years now. I remember quite clearly his generosity and an expression I can describe only as glee that came over him when he would see me or my children, even if he had just seen us a day or two earlier. I can conjure up that expression at will, although we often cannot really remember what someone looks like after a long absence. I remember things he said that hurt me, too, but when the words come back they are disembodied—and that face lit up by love is vivid and personal. When Alison thinks of her mother in five years, or ten—or sooner—perhaps the way she felt when she stroked Beatrice's hair as she fell asleep will stay with her more viscerally than her disappointment that Beatrice didn't understand her better. And perhaps that feeling will be conflated with older memories of Beatrice stroking Alison's hair when Alison was a little girl, before they developed the differences that would separate them later.

To expect ourselves to resolve an entire relationship is unreasonable—just another way to set ourselves up to fail. But *resolve* has many meanings, not just "to find an answer." The word comes from the Latin *solvere*, "to loosen, release," and that is a gentle and comforting way to look at the process that comes at the end of our mothers' lives. First, we loosen the urgency of the push and pull between us; then we open our palms and release them to die in peace.

Mothers and
Daughters: Three
Generations,
circa 1950

My mother, Sarinda
Dranow, and her mother,
my grandmother, Harriet
Staub Cowin, "Skee," with
me, left, and my sister,
Elizabeth, right, in Maine,
where we spent the
summers when we
were young.

Mothers and Daughters: Three Generations, circa 1990

My daughter, Hillary Beard, me, and my mother, with my cairn terrier, Bonnie. After my father died, Mother began to join us for part of each summer.

Afterword:
What Shall We Do about Our Mothers?

When our mothers age and die, they show us how vulnerable we are to the inevitable turns of the life cycle. For members of the baby boom generation, this has a particular poignancy. As the largest cohort in history, baby boomers have had remarkable power to alter social institutions and behavior. We have taken on sex, war, civil rights, and the role of women and changed the way each issue is treated by society.

Now we are sinking our teeth into aging and death—subjects that resist even our massed strength. Perhaps, in an inchoate way, we feel as though we should be able to dodge the final insult that will render us, the invincible generation, into dust, just like everyone who came before.

Those of us who were born after 1940 believe we can take charge, improve, fix, perfect, and more—we feel that it is our obligation to do so. This sense of the perfectibility of life is not just the attitude of modern women and men; it meshes with a traditional American optimism, the belief that anyone can be, do, or have whatever she wants if she just tries hard enough.

We baby boomers have acted on this belief, reinventing ourselves again and again. Through our various resurrections from the ashes of our past selves, we have been unwilling to admit that, at a certain point, we will not be able to reinvent ourselves as young. Age is among the enemies we are determined to vanquish—ours, if not our mothers'.

Women of our mothers' generation are more accepting, less likely to waste energy fighting the inevitable. They lived through the Great Depression, World War II, the use of the atomic bomb—cataclysmic events that humbled those who experienced them. Many of our mothers have now survived the deaths of husbands, siblings, close friends, and sometimes their own children. They know they will follow soon. Their perception of what can be changed is more modest than ours. They do their best within the limitations of luck, opportunity, ability, and time. When the more submissive attitudes of our mothers meet up with our managerial propensities, sometimes we irritate each other.

But it is more than just irritation. Whatever else is out of sync between a woman and her mother, this disjunction between our resistance and their acceptance is a barrier to intimacy and empathy. Age is real; they are old. Our mothers try to accept this reality as best they can; we want to fight it.

Each story I heard from a daughter who asked, "What shall we *do* about our mothers?" set up an echo of voices chanting, "*Do* something." But although we can push back age, we can't eradicate it, even if we live into our hundreds, and our daughters live longer yet. Finally, we will have lived long enough, and we will stop living. Rather than battling this reality, we might do better to change our attitude toward it.

What is called for is empathy, the intuitive connection between mothers and daughters that most of us had when we were young and that many of us lost in the course of establishing our personal and generational identities.

I used to think my mother had eyes in the back of her head (she told me she did) and that she could see me, even if she seemed to be looking away. Such a mother, with the preternatural—or natural—ability to tune in, could save us from peril, destroy us by withholding her love, and reassure her children as no one else could.

She was too powerful, so we tore away some of her power and used it to build our own. Now she has shrunk and lost much of her strength; she can hold us back or propel us forward only if we let her. But she has another power that she can pass along to us: her insider's knowledge of what the end of life looks like.

Empathizing with our mothers and, through them, experiencing endings as well as beginnings is less of a threat than an opportunity. When a mother is too frail to be a heroine or a villain, when her skin becomes soft the way only babies and the very old are soft, we can touch her again.

In a moving essay in the *New York Times Magazine*, Nancy Cobb (who has written about death in her book *In Lieu of Flowers*) describes the intimacy of her last hours with her mother: "I leaned down. She caressed my face. Then, with our cheeks pressed together, our breaths became one—inhale, exhale—rhythmic, elemental, as primitive and natural as labor. We were moving together by way of the spirit, revisiting some distant terrain similar to the one we had shared in silence for nine months." Cobb believes that this connection is "more common than rare . . . bred in the bone . . . deeply embedded in all of us."[1]

The day the essay was published, my mother called me to ask if I had read it. I had. "Beautiful, don't you think?" Mother said. "Yes," I said. Beautiful and devoutly to be wished for.

The more we know about the conditions that can attend old age, the more empathetic we can be—and empathy is the mark of a good daughter.

Can we feel what it is like to be old when we are in the middle of our lives? I think we can. Our mothers ache, forget, mourn, and watch the clock ticking slowly through a long, lonely day, then remind themselves that when the day is over they will be closer to an end that is coming entirely too soon. We have felt that way, too. The difference is that, when we are in midlife, we can realistically expect that our lives will change and that the feelings will subside for a time. We may get married again, have grandchildren, change jobs, plant new gardens, learn to paint or hike. Our mothers have much less to look forward to. We can empathize with their difficulties because we have had similar problems; it is not such a big stretch to imagine how it would feel if we knew that the tough times weren't just temporary.

Women of our generation expend a lot of energy fighting the imperfections that season our lives. It is not easy to be a good daughter to an aging mother; it is not easy to be an aging mother, either. Every stage of life has something to teach us, but to learn, we must be still and listen before we act—and place less emphasis on doing and more on loving. To be responsible is not necessarily to be intrusive. To be companionable does not require constant visits. And love is not canceled out by complex feelings. If we expect only what is reasonable of ourselves and our mothers, we will free ourselves to love them better. Perhaps then we will be less disappointed with ourselves, less angry with them, and less likely to feel guilty.

That said, I can't prevent myself from thinking that a good daughter would have known that railroad tracks were no place for a mother a few months short of her eightieth birthday, who walks with a cane and has a knee that collapses on its own schedule. I did know it. I just didn't want it to be true.

Epilogue: Another Generation
By Hillary Beard

My grandmother, whom I call Cee Cee, once had an elderly mother. I have a picture of my great-grandmother, Skee, cradling me in her lap when I was a baby, a year before she died. Skee's eyes appear youthful and twinkling, delighted with her newest family member. But her hands are knotted and her lap is so sloped that I imagine my mother hovering just outside the frame, ready to catch me in case I wiggled too much.

I know that Skee insisted that her daughter—my grandmother—call her every day, but that is all Cee Cee has told me about Skee's old age. During the research for this book, with all the opportunities for her to tell her own tale of an aging mother, I never heard Cee Cee mention Skee's aging, what happened, or how she felt about it. Cee Cee's generation tended to keep personal matters quieter.

By contrast, women of my mother's generation and my own peers have been eager to talk. As my mother wrote, "Everyone has a story," and given the opportunity to share our stories, we have little reticence. It is as though we have found a collective catharsis in sharing aging mother and grandmother traumas, and we have seized on it.

Women my age, in our midtwenties, have just begun to think about age and death. When I was younger, in grade school, high school, and college, many of my peers' grandparents died. But then it was different. People would disappear from class for a couple of days and return to explain quietly, "My grandfather died."

"I'm so sorry," we might say. "Are you okay?" That was all. Then we moved on to our everyday interests.

Now, as our parents have begun to show signs of aging, our tone has changed.

For many of us, too, our grandmothers are our friends. That may be truer today than it was for earlier generations, who were taught that grandparents were to be treated with a formal, distant respect. And because of societal changes, principally divorce, many of us have become closer to our grandparents than children in two-parent families.

Throughout my own life, I have found friendship, love, and comfort and sought advice from both my grandmothers.

When I was in high school, my father's mother, whom I strongly resemble in looks and behavior, began forgetting things—a state that rapidly disintegrated into senility. True to our friendship, I continued to call her almost every week, and we would have long chats. We seldom ran out of things to talk about, although Granny's end of the conversation could seem a bit surreal. "So how's that brother of yours?" she would ask. I would tell her, in some detail, and then she would pipe in, "That's wonderful. And how's that brother of yours?"

Yet she did remember some of what I told her. Trouble with a boy or in class, a sports injury, or illness usually provoked a follow-up question, sometimes weeks later. "Have you had that shoulder of yours fixed yet?" she would ask, or "How was that test that put you in such a tizzy?"

Watching Granny grow old was the first time I had seen the effects of aging on a close mother figure, and it was defeating. She literally withered: first mentally, then physically, until at the last her spirit shriveled, too.

With Cee Cee, my mother's mother, her mind remains sharp, and I call her often for advice or to cheer me up. But her body is not as strong as her mind. She doesn't eat much, her balance is bad, and her knee buckles without warning. A couple of winters ago, she had a racking cough that wouldn't go away, and she barely left the house. If my phone rang late at night, I often worried that it was bad news. Cee Cee has recovered, but I still wonder what I will hear when the phone rings after midnight.

Because we are close to our grandmothers and mothers, we have a role in their aging. As we hear our mothers fret about their mothers' declines, we participate in ways not so different from a little girl trying to walk in her mother's high heels. The child watches her mother walk, tries on her shoes, makes a successful—or unsuccessful—promenade around the room, and gives the shoes back. With Cee Cee in particular, I have felt the same way: happy that I can carry some of the adult responsibility but relieved that I can put it down at will.

I am very close to Cee Cee, but my role remains mainly that of an observer and advice-giver to my mother. I am more than happy to help, but I live in Washington, while they are in New York. When I am busy with my life, I don't feel that I am shirking a responsibility because I am not around more often.

No matter how close we are to our grandparents, we can keep their aging at arm's length. We help when we're around, during holidays, or more often if our grandparents live in our parents' house. But we can escape. A friend of mine lived at home with his parents and his senile grandmother for six months after graduating from college. "Things are tough around here," he would report. "Nana's driving my father crazy. She keeps trying to feed the dog's heartworm pills to the cat. And it's always my poor mother who has to deal with her." Hearing about Nana's senility and the pressures on my friend's family was unsettling. We felt sorry for his mother and admired her for taking on a difficult responsibility, but mostly we discussed the sometimes hilarious missteps and mistakes of being old. And when my friend began to work, he moved out of his parents' house, to another city, and left his mother and father to deal with Nana.

Still, somewhere in my own slightly distanced watching process, the wheels are turning. When Cee Cee first became frailer, I saw how my mother and aunt dealt with it, each in her own way. I have noticed the shifts in their interdependence and the new tensions and strengths still developing among the three of them. I have been amazed by how much my mother and Cee Cee began to appreciate each other, as mother and daughter, as friends, and as adults—dealing together with the less than ideal situations caused by aging.

But the benefits of Cee Cee's aging are outweighed by the anticipation of bereavement. No matter how good a face you put on it, and no matter how you benefit from new dynamics, the fact remains that a daughter is watching the death march of the person who gave her life. And it is petrifying, no matter how close or distant you are from your mother.

The process of Cee Cee's aging gives me a premonitory glimpse of how my own mother will age. In this way, genes are unfortunate. We see our mothers in our grandmothers—on the road to their own transformation into elderly women. Sometimes, when I see them together, sitting in the living room on summer nights with their dogs and their cups of tea, I see two elderly women, not one, and I hate what I see: wrinkles and sags, white hairs, weakening eyes, older hands, and mannerisms.

This has just begun. I notice it most on the island where we spend our summers, where my friends have known each others' parents all our lives. In the past few years, there have been times when a group of us are sitting around and someone's mother walks by. We silently watch, heads turning in unison, until the person is out of earshot. Then someone might whisper, "She looks so old."

This is the warning bell that has changed my peers' responses. Our mothers are experiencing changes that herald old age. Most have already gone through menopause, a clear gateway to being old. They try to stay fit and to look and feel young, but there is nothing they can do about menopause. They talk to each other about hot flashes, mood swings, and not-understanding relatives. We listen to them and think they don't sound very different from elderly women who complain about bad backs, arthritis—and not-understanding relatives.

My friends' responses to our mothers' physical changes are like those we hear when our mothers talk about our grandmothers. I remember one time when my mother and a friend watched two elderly ladies slowly and unsteadily walking along the beach in their bathing suits. "Will our legs look like that?" my mother's friend asked her, clearly horrified. We, too, are not always understanding or kind about our mothers.

If I honestly described how I see my mother aging, she would be likely to disagree. Just as my grandmother protested that *this book* was making her old, my mother might say that *I* try to make her old. When we go shopping, for example, there are times when I suggest she shouldn't try on something that is too young for her. ("But I *feel* young," she might say.) When she tells me about an adorable guy she met, "He's too young for you," I sometimes say. "Not really," she might hedge.

As grating as it is for us when our mothers seek unnecessary and unbefitting mechanisms to belie their aging, it is more unsettling to note how poorly we often react. As our mothers grow older, they provide regular reminders of their mortality. Our unwillingness to face it and our distaste are like every child's conviction that her parents couldn't possibly have sex. Just as our parents should be chaste, they should also be immortal.

We wish our mothers could stay young forever. Most of us—at least those with loving and attentive mothers—prefer to think of them singing "Rock-a-bye, baby," making cinnamon toast and tea to comfort us when we have the flu, or listening to us sob when relationships end, rather than as women who increasingly need our support. As our mothers begin to fail—physically, mentally, emotionally, or in any other way that compromises their independence and outward strength—daughters are most deeply affected. I certainly am.

My generation has been faced with the fact that our

mothers are fallible early because of some of the choices their generation has made. Many of my friends have single mothers, as I do. We and our mothers are often closer friends. Even for my peers whose mothers are still happily married, the generation gap seems much smaller and our lives more intertwined.

My mother and I are incredibly close. We always have been, even more so after my parents were divorced. Since I was in grade school, my mother and I have discussed my curfew, punishments, and dress; what we'll cook for dinner; and day-to-day minutiae. She is young in spirit and, perhaps because she works with women my age or perhaps because she has a reporter's ear, she has an uncanny grasp of our concerns. There have been innumerable times when my friends come to brunch just to regale my mother with dating and career horrors and to hear her perspective.

I get antsy, however, when my mother shares her own stories—especially about men. It just seems wrong that she should need my advice—that *my mother* might lack the confidence to believe every attractive man would be interested in her. When I was younger, I was positive she had that confidence. I was seven when I went to riding camp in Colorado, and I carried a photograph of my mother to show all the cowboys. I would ask them how old they thought she was. "Isn't she beautiful?" I would preen when they came up with ages at least a decade my mother's junior. I found security in believing that my mother was universally desired, all-comforting, all-knowing, and immortal.

Now I know better. And the flip side of our comfortable closeness is that I know too much. My least favorite phone calls are when my mother needs emotional support and is unhappy or worried, feeling tired or sick, or lonely. I often get impatient and stonewall her, waiting for her to notice that my responses are toneless and short—not exactly the nicest way to return my mother's ever-available ear and shoulder.

It is not just me. Many of our mothers already depend more on us than their mothers did on them. And because our mothers confide in us, we cannot sustain the comforting fiction that they are fine and that we won't have to worry about them for another thirty years. Sometimes when I exaggerate my mother's worries—when, like fingernails on a chalkboard, they sound louder and more harmful to me than they should—I worry that when she really does age, I will be intolerant, impatient, unloving, or ungrateful.

Yet despite these fears, the alternative is worse, as I realized when talking to a friend whose mother had recently died in her fifties. He said he would give up a great deal to help his mother grow old and related a scene he saw in a restaurant that encapsulated his feelings: a middle-aged man was having dinner with his elderly mother, who was disabled by Parkinson's disease. My friend was struck less by the effort required to attend to the mother's needs than by the son's sweetness, tenderness, and patience. He said that, as he watched them, he wished for those extra years with his mother, no matter the burden.

I understand the way he feels. Neither I nor my peers— nor my mother—can imagine life without our mothers.

Now that the generation that came of age in the 1960s has opened the gates to more open discussion about each stage of life, other women, for generations to come, will sit around and discuss their mothers' aging. They can draw strength from each other and from knowing they are not alone. My generation is lucky in that way. Unlike women brought up, as Cee Cee was, in the 1920s, who didn't openly talk about how their mothers' aging affected them, we discuss age with our mothers, with our grandmothers, and among ourselves. Unlike our mothers, who learned later that it is okay to discuss these things, we have already begun. That doesn't mean it won't be difficult for us, too, to be good daughters when our mothers age, but we will have had the chance to learn from the experiences they have chosen to share with us.

Women all around us, friends and strangers, face the same problems, tell their personal stories, and listen to one another. Through this sharing, the solidarity of generations can emerge. My mother and her friends help each other find the strength to care for their mothers, and their examples help prepare us to take our turn. We are beginning to wonder how to prepare ourselves to care for our mothers, making tea and cinnamon toast to soothe the person who soothed us. Luckily, because our mothers' generation has shown us the catharsis of talking more openly, we may even be able to ask them.

I still fear that I will be inadequate at taking care of my mother, as I am now. But I know that she'll try to understand and that she hates growing old as much as I don't want her to. I have noticed, too, that my mother is tougher than I thought. She can take it when I "make her feel old." She *does* take it when I don't really listen to her needs and wants. And she understands when I am crabby at her for needing me.

It seems appropriate that the granddaughter of the subject and the daughter of the author should provide this book's closing words. As the book formed, and as it became clear that my mother was not just using it to make sense of her own relationship with her mother, mine has been almost a bird's-eye view. It is not yet my time to support my mother. But she has brought the topic into our family early enough for me to start figuring it out. It is like discussing your wedding ideas well before the groom shows up: there is much less pressure, so we can explore shifting and often conflicting dynamics. I have learned a great deal from watching my mother. I am neither the subject nor the object of this book, yet, I am the beneficiary. *Good Daughters* has been bequeathed to me by my mother. As she wrote, she created a legacy and a gift. In my mind, it is mainly for me. But it is also a gift to my peers, to my mother's peers, to her mother, and to her mother's peers. I thank her for that.

Notes

INTRODUCTION

1. Bureau of the Census, "65+ in the United States," Current Population Reports, Special Studies, P23–190 (Washington, D.C., 1996), 2–3.

2. Ibid., 2-2.

3. Bureau of the Census, *Statistical Brief, Sixty-five Plus in the United States*, SB/95-8 (Washington, D.C., 1995).

4. Ibid.

5. Bureau of the Census, "65+ in the United States," 2–19.

6. Ibid., vi.

7. Bureau of the Census, *Statistical Brief, Sixty-five Plus in the United States*.

CHAPTER 1

1. Victoria Secunda, *When You and Your Mother Can't Be Friends: Resolving the Most Complicated Relationship of Your Life* (New York: Delta/Bantam Doubleday Dell, 1990), 61.

2. Jan Cohn, *Covers of the Saturday Evening Post* (New York: Viking Studio Books, 1995).

3. This ad appeared in 1950s issues of *Town & Country* magazine.

4. Secunda, *When You and Your Mother Can't Be Friends*, 62.

5. U.S. Department of Labor, Bureau of Labor Statistics, "Household Data, Annual Averages, Employment status of the civilian noninstitutional population by age, sex, and race" [online table], ftp://ftp.bls.gov/pub/special.requests/lf/aat3.txt.

6. Ibid.

7. U.S. Census Bureau, The Official Statistics, Historical Income Tables—Persons, "Table P-4. Race and Hispanic Origin—All Persons 15 Years

Old and Over, by Median and Mean Income: 1947 to 1996" [online table], http://www.census.gov/hhes/income/histinc/p04.html.

8. Bureau of the Census, "65+ in the United States," 4–17.

9. Melinda Beck et al., "The Daughter Track," *Newsweek*, 16 July 1990.

10. Department of the Census, "Table A-1. Years of School Completed by People 25 Years Old and Over, by Age and Gender: Selected Years 1940 to 1997" [online table], http://www.census.gov/population/socdemo/education/tablea-01.txt.

11. Centers for Disease Control, Fastats A to Z, "Marriage," http://www.cdc.gov/nchswww/fastats/marriage.htm.

12. Bureau of the Census, Current Population Survey (Washington, D.C., March 1996).

13. Beck et al., "The Daughter Track."

14. Eugene Aronowitz and Eleanor Mallach Bromberg, eds., *Mental Health and Aging* (Canton, Mass.: Prodist/Watson Publishing, 1986), 54.

15. Ibid., 70.

16. *Family Caregiving in the U.S.: Findings from a National Survey* (Washington, D.C.: National Alliance for Caregiving and American Association of Retired Persons, 1997), 18.

17. Beck et al., "The Daughter Track."

18. Administration on Aging, "Elderaction: Action Ideas for Older Persons and Their Families," http://www.aoa.dhhs.gov/aoa/eldractn/caregive.html.

19. Bureau of the Census, Current Population Reports, P23–180.

20. U.S. Department of Labor, "Household Data, Annual Averages, Employment status of the civilian noninstitutional population by age, sex, and racc."

CHAPTER 2

1. Interview with Helen E. Fisher.

2. Sir James G. Frazer, *The Golden Bough* (New York: Macmillan, 1958), 456.

3. Edith Hamilton, *Mythology* (New York: Penguin, 1969), 29.

CHAPTER 3

1. Mary Pipher, *Reviving Ophelia: Saving the Selves of Adolescent Girls* (New York: Random House, 1994), 54, 57.

2. Katie Couric interviews Emma Thompson and Phyllida Law, *Today*, 31 December 1997, National Broadcasting Company.

3. Anne Rivers Siddons, *Up Island* (New York: HarperCollins, 1997), 67.

4. Interview with Helen E. Fisher.

Notes

CHAPTER 4

1. Sara Rimer, "Rural Elderly Create Vital Communities as Young Leave Void," *New York Times*, 2 February 1998.

2. Robert N. Butler, M.D., *Why Survive? Being Old in America* (New York: Harper & Row, 1985), 4.

3. Bureau of the Census, "65+ in the United States," 3–14.

4. National Institute on Aging, Age Page, "Hearing and Older People," http://www.nih.gov/nia/health/pubpub/hearing.htm.

5. P. F. Adams and M. A. Marano, "Current Estimates from the National Health Interview Survey, 1994," *National Center for Health Statistics Vital Health Statistics* 10, no. 193 (1995): 83–84.

6. Ibid.

7. National Institute on Aging, Age Page, "Osteoporosis: The Silent Bone Thinner," http://www.nih.gov/nia/health/pubpub/osteo.htm.

8. National Institute on Aging, Age Page, "Urinary Incontinence," http://www.nih.gov/nia/health/pubpub/urinary. htm.

9. Centers for Disease Control, Office of Women's Health, "Health in Later Years," http://www.cdc.gov/od/owh/whily.htm.

10. National Institute on Aging, "Progress Report on Alzheimer's Disease, 1997," http://www.alzheimers.org/pr97.html#prevalence.

11. Adams and Marano, "Current Estimates from the National Health Interview Survey, 1994."

12. Ibid.

13. Bureau of the Census, "65+ in the United States," 4–12.

14. John W. Rowe, M.D. and Robert L. Kahn, Ph.D., *Successful Aging* (New York: Random House, 1998).

15. Sara Rimer, "An Aging Nation Ill-Equipped for Hanging Up the Car Keys," *New York Times*, 15 December 1997.

16. Interview with Christine Cassell.

17. *Family Caregiving in the U.S.*, 16.

18. National Institute on Aging, Age Page, "Crime and Older People," http://www.nih.gov/nia/health/pubpub/crime.htm.

19. Interview with Robert Butler.

20. Interview with Rose Dobrof.

21. Bureau of the Census, "65+ in the United States," 6–2.

22. Butler, *Why Survive? Being Old in America*.

23. Interview with Rose Dobrof.

24. Interview with Christine Cassell.

25. Interview with Rose Dobrof.

CHAPTER 5

1. Butler, *Why Survive? Being Old in America*, 372.

2. Ibid.

3. Interview with Robert Butler.

4. Ibid.
5. Ibid.
6. Interview with Rose Dobrof.

CHAPTER 6

1. Butler, *Why Survive? Being Old in America*, 225.
2. Ibid., 408.
3. Interview with Robert Butler.
4. Interview with Rose Dobrof.

CHAPTER 7

1. Interview with Rose Dobrof.

CHAPTER 8

1. Victor G. Cicirelli, *Helping Elderly Parents: The Role of Adult Children* (Boston: Auburn House, 1981), 69.
2. Interview with Helen E. Fisher.
3. Interview with Christine Cassell.

CHAPTER 11

1. Wendy Gimbel, "Kalala's Doll," *Parnassus* 16, no. 2 (1991).

CHAPTER 12

1. *Family Caregiving in the U.S.*
2. Eric Pace, "Benjamin Spock, World's Pediatrician, Dies at 94," *New York Times*, 17 March 1998, B10.

CHAPTER 16

1. Sara Rimer, "Blacks Carry Load of Care for Their Elderly," *New York Times*, 15 March 1998.

CHAPTER 17

1. Elisabeth Kübler-Ross, M.D., *On Death and Dying* (New York: Simon & Schuster, 1997).
2. Marie de Hennezel, *Intimate Death* (New York: Alfred A. Knopf, 1997), 111–12.
3. Ibid., 60–61.
4. Ibid., 70.
5. Ibid., 159.
6. Ibid., 182.

Notes

AFTERWORD

1. Nancy Cobb, "Last Communion," *New York Times Magazine*, 15 March 1998, 88.

Bibliography

Apter, Terri. *Altered Loves: Mothers and Daughters During Adolescence*. New York: Fawcett-Columbine/Ballantine Books, 1990.

Aronowitz, Eugene, and Eleanor Mallach Bromberg, eds. *Mental Health and Aging*. Canton, Mass.: Prodist/Watson Publishing, 1986.

Beauvoir, Simone de. *The Coming of Age*. New York: G.P. Putnam's Sons, 1972.

Benjamin, Jessica. *The Bonds of Love: Psychoanalysis, Feminism, and the Problem of Domination*. New York: Pantheon Books, 1988.

Berg, Elizabeth. *What We Keep*. New York: Random House, 1998.

Bloomfield, Harold H., M.D., with Leonard Felder, Ph.D. *Making Peace with Your Parents*. New York: Random House, 1983.

Bromberg, Eleanor Mallach. "Mother Daughter Relationships in Later Life: Negating the Myths." In *Mental Health and Aging*, ed. Eugene Aronowitz and Eleanor Mallach Bromberg. Canton, Mass.: Prodist/Watson Publishing, 1986.

Butler, Robert N., M.D. *Why Survive? Being Old in America*. New York: Harper & Row, 1985.

Butler, Robert N., M.D., Myrna Lewis, and Trey Sunderland. *Aging and Mental Health, Positive Psychosocial and Biomedical Approaches*. New York: Merrill/Macmillan, 1991.

Cicirelli, Victor G. *Helping Elderly Parents: The Role of Adult Children*. Boston: Auburn House, 1981.

Cohn, Jan. *Covers of the Saturday Evening Post*. New York: Viking Studio Books, 1995.

Cowen, Lauren, and Jayne Waxler. *Daughters and Mothers*. Philadelphia: Running Press, 1997.

Bibliography

Dobrof, Rose. "Stress on Families." In *Mental Health and Aging*, ed. Eugene Aronowitz and Eleanor Mallach Bromberg. Canton, Mass.: Prodist/Watson Publishing, 1986.

Frazer, Sir James G. *The Golden Bough*. New York: Macmillan, 1958.

Friday, Nancy. *My Mother, Myself: The Daughter's Search for Identity*. New York: Delacorte Press, 1977.

Hamilton, Edith. *Mythology*. New York: Penguin, 1969.

Hennezel, Marie de. *Intimate Death*. New York: Alfred A. Knopf, 1997.

Jonas, Susan, and Marilyn Nissenson. *Friends for Life: Enriching the Bond between Mothers and Their Adult Daughters*. New York: Harcourt Brace, 1997.

Kübler-Ross, Elisabeth, M.D. *On Death and Dying*. New York: Simon & Schuster, 1997.

Martz, Sandra Haldeman, ed. *When I Am an Old Woman I Shall Wear Purple*. Watsonville, Calif.: Papier-Mache Press, 1997.

Otto, Whitney. *How to Make an American Quilt*. New York: Ballantine Books, 1992.

Pipher, Mary, Ph.D. *Reviving Ophelia: Saving the Selves of Adolescent Girls*. New York: Random House, 1994.

Rowe, John W., M.D., and Robert L. Kahn, Ph.D. *Successful Aging*. New York: Random House, 1998.

Saline, Carol, and Sharon J. Wohlmuth. *Mothers and Daughters*. New York: Doubleday, 1997.

Scarf, Maggie. *Unfinished Business: Pressure Points in the Lives of Women*. New York: Doubleday, 1980.

Scileppi, Kenneth P., M.D. *Caring for the Parents Who Cared for You: What to Do When an Aging Parent Needs You*. Seacaucus, N.J.: Birch Lane Press/Carol Publishing, 1996.

Secunda, Victoria. *When You and Your Mother Can't Be Friends: Resolving the Most Complicated Relationship of Your Life*. New York: Delta/Bantam Doubleday Dell, 1990.

Sheehy, Gail. *New Passages: Mapping Your Life across Time*. New York: Random House, 1995.

Siddons, Anne Rivers. *Up Island*. New York: HarperCollins, 1997.

Stern, Daniel N. *The Motherhood Constellation: A Unified View of Parent-Infant Psychotherapy*. New York: Basic Books/ HarperCollins, 1995.

Troll, Lillian E., Sheila J. Miller, and Robert C. Atchley. *Families in Later Life*. Belmont, Calif.: Wadsworth, 1979.

Waterhouse, Debra. *Like Mother, Like Daughter: How Women Are Influenced by Their Mothers' Relationship with Food—and How to Break the Pattern*. New York: Hyperion, 1997.

PERIODICALS AND TELEVISION

Beck, Melinda, with Barbara Kantrowitz and Lucille Beachy in New York, Mary Hager in Washington, Jeanne Gordon in Los Angeles, Elizabeth

BIBLIOGRAPHY

Roberts in Miami, and Roxie Hammill in Kansas City. "The Daughter Track." *Newsweek*, 16 July 1990.

"Boomers! The Babies Face Fifty." *Modern Maturity*, January–February 1996.

Brody, Jane E. "Grand Examples of the Right Stuff for Aging Well." *New York Times*, 21 April 1998.

———. "Older Women Often Get Caught in a Bottleneck with Managed Care." *New York Times*, 13 August 1997.

———. "When a Dying Patient Seeks Suicide Aid, It May Be a Signal to Fight Depression." *New York Times*, 18 June 1997.

Cobb, Nancy. "Last Communion." *New York Times Magazine*, 15 March 1998.

Conover, Ted. "The Last Nanny." *New York Times Magazine*, 30 November 1997.

Fein, Esther B. "Failing to Discuss Dying Adds to Pain of Patient and Family." *New York Times*, 5 March 1997.

Flaherty, Julie. "Where Retirement Became a Dirty Word." *New York Times*, 28 December 1997.

Foderano, Lisa W. "Death Wishes." *New York Times*, 3 April 1994.

"Funny, We Don't Feel Old." *New York Times Magazine*, themed issue, 9 March 1997.

Gilbert, Susan. "Elderly Seek Longer Life, Regardless." *New York Times*, 10 February 1998.

Gimbel, Wendy. "Kalala's Doll." *Parnassus* 16, no. 2 (1991).

Lewin, Tamar. "Women Losing Ground to Men in Widening Income Difference." *New York Times*, 15 September 1997.

Loewenstein, Sophie Freud. "Mother and Daughter—an Epitaph." *Family Process* 20 (March 1981): 3ff.

Lyall, Sarah. "Like Mother, Like Daughter, and Acted Out." *New York Times*, 21 December 1997.

Miller, Judith. "When Foundations Chime In, the Issue of Dying Comes to Life." *New York Times*, 22 November 1997.

O'Connor, Amy. "Why Grandma, What Smooth Skin You Have!" *Mirabella*, March–April 1998.

Oser, Alan S. "New York Area Retirees Get More Housing Choices." *New York Times*, 10 May 1998.

Pace, Eric. "Benjamin Spock, World's Pediatrician, Dies at 94." *New York Times*, 17 March 1998, B10.

Page, Margot. "Go Gently." *American Health*, October 1988.

"Poll Looks at Innermost Feelings About Life's End." *New York Times*, 6 December 1997.

Rimer, Sara. "Families Bear a Bigger Share of Long-Term Care for the Frail Elderly." *New York Times*, 8 June 1998, A18.

———. "New Needs for Retirement Complexes' Oldest." *New York Times*, 23 March 1998.

———. "Blacks Carry Load of Care for Their Elderly." *New York Times*, 15 March 1998, 1.

———. "Rural Elderly Create Vital Communities as Young Leave Void." *New York Times*, 2 February 1998, 1ff.

———. "An Aging Nation Ill-Equipped for Hanging Up the Car Keys." *New York Times*, 15 December 1997, 1ff.

Rosenbaum, David E. "A Senator's Old Speech Holds Truths for Today (Mike Mansfield at 95)." *New York Times*, 22 March 1998.

Shute, Nancy. "Why Do We Age?" *U.S. News & World Report*, 18–25 August 1997.

Smith, Roberta. "Beatrice Wood, 105, Potter and Mama of Dada, Is Dead." *New York Times*, 14 March 1998.

Stern, Jonathan, M.D. "A Cognitive Appraisal Approach to Parent Training with Affect-Driven Parents." *Psychotherapy* 33, no. 1 (spring 1996): 77ff.

Stolberg, Sheryl Gay. "Embracing a Right to Die Well." *New York Times*, 19 June 1997.

Today. Katie Couric interviews Emma Thompson and Phyllida Law, 31 December 1997, National Broadcasting Company.

"A Valuable Guide to Successful Aging." *New York Times*, 14 April 1998.

Witt, Karen de. "Burning at Both Ends, Boomers Turn 50." *New York Times*, 13 November 1996.

PUBLICATIONS BY GOVERNMENT AND PRIVATE ORGANIZATIONS (INCLUDING INTERNET PUBLICATIONS)

Adams, P. R., and M. A. Marano. "Current Estimates from the National Health Interview Survey, 1994." *National Center for Health Statistics Vital Health Statistics* 10, no. 193 (1995).

Administration on Aging. "Elderaction: Action Ideas for Older Persons and Their Families," http://www.aoa.dhhs.gov/aoa/eldractn/caregive.html.

Brody, Elaine M. "The Etiquette of Filial Behavior." Paper presented at "Old Age Values and Prospects," a conference sponsored by the Philadelphia Geriatric Center and the Stephen Smith Home for the Aged, York House South, Philadelphia, 13 October 1979.

Bureau of the Census. "65+ in the United States." Current Population Reports, Special Studies, P23-190, Washington, D.C., 1996.

———. *Sixty-five Plus in the United States, Statistical Brief* SB/95-8, Washington, D.C., May 1995.

———. Current Population Survey. Washington, D.C., March 1996.

———. Current Population Reports, Series P-60, Income Statistics Branch/ HHES Division. Washington, D.C.

———. Current Population Reports, Series P-60, Income Statistics Branch/ HHES Division, U.S. Bureau of the Census, U.S. Department of Commerce, Washington, D.C.

Family Caregiving in the U.S.: Findings from a National Survey. Washington, D.C.: National Alliance for Caregiving and the American Association of Retired Persons, 1997.

BIBLIOGRAPHY

National Institute on Aging. Age Page, "Crime and Older People," http://www.nih.gov/nia/health/pubpub/hearing.htm.

———. Age Page, "Hearing and Older People," http://www.nih.gov/nia/health/pubpub/hearing.htm.

———. Age Page, "Osteoporosis: The Silent Bone Thinner," http://www.nih.gov/nia/health/pubpub/osteo.htm.

——— Age Page, "Urinary Incontinence," http://www.nih.gov/nia/health/pubpub/urinary.htm.

———. "Progress Report on Alzheimer's Disease, 1997," http://www.alzheimers.org/pr97.html#prevalence.

U.S. Department of Health and Human Services, Centers for Disease Control, Fastats A to Z, "Marriage," http://www.cdc.gov/nchswww/fastats/marriage.htm.

U.S. Department of Health and Human Services, Centers for Disease Control, Office of Women's Health, "Health in Later Years," http://www.cdc.gov/od/owh/whily.htm.

U.S. Department of Labor. Household Data, Annual Averages, "Table A-3. Employment Status of the Civilian Noninstitutional Population by Age, Sex, and Race" [online table], ftp://ftp.bls.gov/pub/special.requests/lf/aat3.txt.

CONFERENCE

"Countdown to 2000: Baby Boomers Face the New Millennium," sponsored by The Hebrew Home for the Aged at Riverdale and Brookdale Center on Aging of Hunter College, New York, 15 September 1997.

INTERVIEWS

In addition to the interviews with hundreds of daughters, who are not credited by name to preserve their privacy, I interviewed the following:

Susan Burden, psychologist.

Robert N. Butler, M.D., Director, the International Longevity Institute.

Christine Cassell, M.D., Professor and Chairman, Henry L. Schwarz Department of Geriatrics & Adult Development, Mount Sinai Medical Center.

Rose Dobrof, Ph.D., cofounder of the Brookdale Center on Aging of Hunter College.

Helen E. Fisher, anthropologist.

Harry R. Moody, Ph.D., cofounder and executive director of the Brookdale Center on Aging of Hunter College.

Gillian Walker, Ph.D.

Many of the initial stories that were developed further for profiles or shorter anecdotes initially came through a roundtable conducted by the psychologist Sheenah Hankin, Ph.D., which she held at her home in July 1997. Sheenah helped me review and interpret the transcripts, and read and commented on an early draft of some of the stories. Her training, intuition, and common sense helped me avoid the traps of psychological fads and encouraged me to take a more humanist approach to evaluating the situations. Any errors or misinterpretations are my own.

Richard Wessler, Ph.D., also reviewed and commented on an early draft of some stories.

Acknowledgments

The following people have contributed time, intelligence, and heart to this enterprise.

Amy Einhorn, my editor at Warner Books, made the leap of faith and then suggested incisive editorial improvements that both tightened and expanded the prose and the ideas in *Good Daughters*. I have been fortunate to work with her.

Sheenah Hankin generously presided over a roundtable discussion at her home, to which she invited many of the women whose stories I have told. Sheenah's insights helped me develop a way of thinking about their relationships.

Many, many women have told me their stories. Their lives are at the core of this book. Chief among them are the women who attended the roundtable discussion, filled in questionnaires, and answered follow-up questions. They know who they are.

Rose Dobrof, of the Brookdale Center on Aging, helped direct my thinking long before I had written a book proposal, and submitted to a very long interview. Her warmth and intelligence have been inspiring.

Harry R. Moody consulted and encouraged me at the same early stage.

Robert Butler, the dean of the field of aging, made time for an important and substantive interview.

Christine Cassell, of the Mount Sinai Medical Center, also set aside time to answer questions.

Hannah Schneider, who is both my cousin and an accomplished expert in gerontology, opened doors to helpful information.

Helen E. Fisher answered questions from an anthropologist's point of view when she was on deadline for her own book.

I have neither met nor interviewed Marie de Hennezel, but her book, *Intimate Death*, guided my approach to the process of "attending" someone who is dying.

Sara Rimer's articles on aging in the *New York Times* are among the best writing on aspects of this subject.

Ellen Warner's superb cover photograph and portrait of me and my mother have given me keepsakes of our island summers.

Jean Calhoun and David Rubitski provided equipment and spent time to help me work out the cover photograph.

Carrie Hall transcribed interviews and made helpful comments on drafts.

These friends and relatives have provided moral support, hospitality, and encouragement: Alexandra Anderson-Spivy, who read the entire first draft with a sharp pencil and a sharp mind; Sam Anson and Peter Beard, and the late Roseanne H. Beard; Dana Cowin; David Cowin;

ACKNOWLEDGMENTS

Lynn Foster; Lorna and Ed Goodman; Bob and Jane Patterson; Elaina Richardson; Molly Schaefer and Dan Slott; Lois Farfel Stark, my oldest friend and a remarkable sounding board; and Ann Thorne.

P<small>ATRICIA</small> B<small>EARD</small> is a contributing writer to *Elle, Town &
Country*, and *Mirabella*, and her articles have appeared in
many national magazines. She is the author of *Growing
Up Republican*, a biography of Christine Todd Whitman,
the first woman governor of New Jersey.